the
Hyperactive
Child

the Hyperactive Child

Domeena C. Renshaw, M.D.

Nelson-Hall
nh Chicago

To:

Troubled children on their long journey

ISBN: 0–911012–76–1

Library of Congress Catalog Card No. 73–86936

Copyright © 1974 by Domeena C. Renshaw, M.D.

Third printing, 1977

Manufactured in the United States of America.

Contents

	Foreword	vii
1	Introduction	1
2	The Hyperactive Child	9
3	The Hyperanxious Child	29
4	The Hyperaggressive Child	45
5	Discipline	57
6	The Hyperkinetic Child— Definition and Diagnosis	77
7	The Hyperkinetic Child— Epidemiology, Pathology and Work-up	95
8	The Hyperkinetic Child— Management and Treatment	111
9	The Hyperkinetic Child— Medications	133
10	The Hyperkinetic Child— Prognosis and Prevention	161
11	Epilogue	175
	Bibliography	179
	Index	189

Foreword

In this very readable monograph, Dr. Renshaw has managed to impart a great deal of information derived from clinical and experimental investigation and to blend it with the sympathy for children and their families, the wisdom born of clinical experience and the ability to teach which characterize the good physician. "The Hyperactive Child" is an appropriate title because it is a book about children, rather than just about a disease syndrome. Thus, it sets in proper perspective what has been recognized in recent years as probably a specific neurophysiologic disturbance, manifested by a high degree of distractibility, over-responsiveness to stimuli and a paradoxically tranquillizing reaction to stimulants of the dexedrine-benzedrine series of drugs. I say "probably a specific neurophysiologic disturbance," because since, like dyslexia (specific language disability), it is a non-fatal condition, peculiar to man, from which many children recover or, at least, to which they adjust successfully as they grow up, there has been no way to study the disturbances of anatomy or physiology suspected as being responsible. Nevertheless, the clinical picture of the two conditions is specific enough, and the response to special treatment sufficiently dramatic, to make one feel that, in the majority of instances, the hyperkinetic child or the dyslexic child is suffering from a disturbance of neurological functioning which has a definite anatomic or biochemical basis.

As Dr. Renshaw points out, hyperactivity is a common symptom, seen in many children, which must be evaluated against the background of their mental and neurological development, as well as their home and school environments, but it is only the ceaseless, purposeless, uncontrollable hyperactivity characterizing the specific syndrome that responds so unexpectedly and frequently to dexedrine. Since estimates of this latter condition run as high as 10% of all children, it is clearly a major clinical problem for parents, pediatricians and teachers. This book is written to inform the professionals, as well as to help parents. Above all, it is written with deep sympathy for the children, who are either the victims of this disorder or of the constraints of modern life which may make even normally active child behavior socially unacceptable. Every educated person dealing with children will find much in this book by a dedicated physician that will be helpful in their daily lives and work.

Charles A. Janeway, M.D.
Children's Hospital Medical Center
Harvard University

The child is father to the man

William Wordsworth

1

Introduction

"The child is father to the man." Thus, long before Freud, wrote an English poet. It is no longer news that all of us are profoundly affected by our early years, yet memory plays strange tricks, and we forget what it was like to be a child. Today we see children as a special group, quite separate from adults. This concept of the separateness of children is a relatively new one, dating from the last four centuries. Before this time, boys and girls shared beds, meals, clothes, chores, and diversions with their elders.

The first to be separated from adults were sons and daughters of the well-to-do, followed by the middle class, and finally the working class. This division is also peculiarly specific to Western culture. The large majority of mankind has treated children simply as younger members of society, not equal, but not separate. Children have always contrived to form a subculture of their own,

1

their games in ancient Athens, modern Europe, New York, and Asia all showing definite similarity to each other.

It must be remembered that infants prior to the 18th and 19th centuries died more frequently than they lived. Until they had reached the end of infancy and survived to about the age of seven, they were scarcely counted. Life was too harsh for society to be overconcerned about an infant who probably would not survive anyway. However, from the 17th century, the child became an object of respect, recognized as having a different nature and different needs, requiring separation and "protection" from the adult world.

Scholars, particularly the Jesuits, who dominated education of the aristocracy and the rich middle class, influenced the manners and morals of children, beginning a revolution in cultural attitudes toward learning in children. Many of the basic assumptions regarding formal schooling that are regarded today as belonging to human nature itself were adopted during this time, for example: beginning the processes of a literate education with teaching reading at about four or five along with writing, arithmetic and then gradually proceeding to more complex subjects.

Education is now tied automatically to the calendar age of children in the modern world. With rapid changes in society, and the advance of science, technology, and industry, increasing demands are made upon members of Western society for obtaining training in specific skills and for better and higher education. With urbanization and population pressures, schools become larger, more complex, and more structured. Individual classrooms contain more children for long hours, with a standard workload that seems to increase with each passing year.

Although the 20th century is recognized as the age of the emergent individual, it has also demanded increased conformity of the individual child to the subculture of the classroom. Little latitude exists in the modern schoolroom for deviant behavior of even moderate degree. It is not surprising, therefore, that the greatest peak of recognition of the "hyperactive" child is between five and seven years of age, when the child is expected to conform to the norms of other children of his own age in the kindergarten or first grade setting. It is entirely expectable and quite appropriate that teachers should recognize and attempt to assist the excessively hyperactive child, since otherwise the disruption of the larger group will create a less-than-optimum milieu for all concerned.

The label "hyperkinetic child" has appeared frequently in educational, scientific, and general literature since the 1950s. It has been overused, ambiguously used, incorrectly used. Estimates have appeared stating that there are three million hyperkinetic children in the United States, that 7% of all school children are hyperkinetic, that 4% of pediatric practice consists of hyperkinetic children.

Ambiguity and exaggeration have resulted from lack of clear definition in description and diagnosis of this condition. Since the 1940s, many workers in the field of medicine began to demonstrate the effects of organic brain disorders on the behavior and psychological function of children, showing a spectrum from severe to minor dys-

3

functions. In the 1950s, the concept of "minimal brain dys-function" became popular, with a tendency to over-simplify and overgeneralize the concept, disregarding diagnostic essentials. In 1954, at the International Insti-tute on Child Psychiatry in Toronto, Canada, Dr. Maurice W. Laufer, M.D., who had worked in collaboration with Denhoff and Solomons, read a paper entitled "Hyperkinetic Impulse Disorder in Children's Behavior Problems," signalling a turning point away from vague generalities to more specific definition.

It is the aim of this book to point out that not every child who wriggles is necessarily hyperkinetic. Unfortu-nately there has been much confusion. Some synonyms have compounded rather than relieved ambiguity. There is also a lack of agreement in the literature, as well as misinterpretation of outlined categories. Thirty-eight terms such as "minimal brain damage", "minimal cerebral dysfunction", "minimal brain dysfunction", hyperkinetic syndrome", "hyperactive child", "impulse disorder", etc., were found in a National Institute of Mental Health, (NIMH) study. All were used to describe children with ex-aggerated overactivity.

Hyperactivity is a symptom. Hyperkinetic "syn-drome" (HK) is a collection of clinical *behavioral* manifes-tations, forming a clinical entity with a wide spectrum from mild to severe. *Minimal Brain Dysfunction* (MBD) describes the phenomena of disturbances of cognition, perception, and learning, which is commonly seen in this condition. *Minimal Brain Damage* is a term attempting to describe presumptive underlying pathology within the

4

brain of the child, which might have occurred in utero, during delivery, or during early life. All workers in this field agree that much study is yet to be done for completeness of understanding and definition of the widely divergent group of children covered by these definitions.

An attempt is made in these pages to clarify existing data. The child should be assisted from the earliest possible time along the long and bumpy road he will have to travel while he attempts to attain his optimum potential at all levels. Understanding the difficulties can greatly assist all auxilliary adults in their ongoing daily challenge of coping with the irregular and frequently explosive behavior of these special children, as they variously grow and develop, each within his or her special abilities or disabilities.

It is logical to believe that historically the hyperkinetic child has always been with us. Literature, children's verses and anecdotes confirm this. However, for reasons described earlier in this chapter, his recognition as a specific clinical entity had not been documented until the recent past. The outlook today is one which offers encouragement and hope. By careful study it has been established that there are many helps for the child, as well as for the family and school. Clearer understanding will give better management. Medications that control a great deal of the unacceptable behavior are now in wide use. Fuller understanding of the nature of the condition will allow for maintenance and follow-up which can give continuing improvement in function at educational, personal, and social levels for child, family, and school.

I know a person small—
He keeps ten million serving men
Who get no rest at all!
He sends 'em abroad on his own affairs
From the second he opens his eyes—
One million Hows, two million Wheres,
And seven million Whys!

Rudyard Kipling

2

The Hyperactive Child

Movement, sound and activity are indicators of the life process at all levels in the animal kingdom. If one considers the birth process of the human infant, one remembers the life-saving significance of the screaming and stretching of the neonate.

In the baby, motor movements such as sucking, stretching, smiling, sitting, and standing are regarded as predictable milestones of normal growth and development. Before the development of language, and therefore of social responses, movement is closely observed and eagerly encouraged by parents who show pride in their infant, taking special joy when the child gurgles, reaches out, flips his little body around, sits, kicks, and begins to crawl.

There is a great deal of almost ceaseless waving of the arms and kicking of the legs in the waking periods of the life of the pre-ambulant baby. Once there is maturity of

9

the central nervous system which is adequate to control the weight of the child in the sitting, standing, and walking postures, independent movement becomes possible, and then repetitively practiced.

Almost synchronous with independent movement, language evolves—from babbling sounds to clearly recognized words, small phrases, and then sentences. There is ceaseless repetition of new words, as the toddler begins to master the simultaneous developing skills of motor control and speech. All the while he integrates the numerous visual, tactile, and auditory stimuli received from his hours of gazing, listening, touching, and contemplation of people and objects around.

It is therefore stressed that overactivity, restlessness, and distractibility occur *normally* as part of phase-related growth and development in the infant and in the young pre-school child before the age of four or five. In older children under stress, with excitement or fatigue, emotional tension may be discharged as hyperactivity. Excess chattering, restlessness, and distractibility are usually easily accepted as mild regression in the response to such situations. This reactive hyperactivity usually clears up rapidly, and appropriate phase-related behavior returns when conditions normalize.

If hyperactivity persists when the child is already of school-going age, it may be regarded as a sign of "immaturity" or poor social skills, representing either inability or unwillingness to learn control of motor and verbal impulses. If such immature patterns of excessive uncontrolled, unsocialized motor and verbal behavior continue after the age of eight, they are considered more definitely pathological and will require further study and some form of modification.

Play is regarded as the "work of the child", through which he imitates and patterns behavior, practices and masters difficult situations, and uses make-believe to conquer frightening concepts. Play is an essential human ability to use the skill of imagination in setting up model situations for mastery through safe fantasy and factual experimentation. Like many other young animals, the child playfully and vigorously exercises every muscle in his body, including his vocal cords, and thus achieves better co-ordination and control. In the sanctuary of the home, where the child is at ease and not as inhibited as in the classroom, there is greater freedom for outlet and expression of both muscular and verbal needs.

Behavior appropriate in the classroom is gradually taught and encouraged by parents, older siblings, and then in the direct schoolroom situation. As the child adjusts to the strangeness of the classroom, he may show increased distractibility and restlessness during the first month. With some children, there may be a need to show off and clown as they establish their position in the local power structure. Gradually this status struggle settles down. Variations of expectable behavior for kindergarten or first grade will depend upon the authoritarianism or liberalism of the particular culture and of the individual teacher.

In Western culture, particularly in the United States, free expression and development of an individual are highly prized. There are few servants. Mothers are involved in the direct care of the children as well as of the home, and frequently hold an outside job as well. The old dictum "children should be seen and not heard" rarely prevails, although some families do perpetuate child-rearing practices from generations past. While some babies are left for a number of years in a playpen, this is the exception rather than the rule, since most commercial equipment for babies is directed toward motility and muscle co-ordination.

Ceaseless activity, constant noise, a high need for distraction and stimulation are recognized and accepted in the two-year-old or even up to four years old by most young mothers. The capacity to sustain attention long enough to watch an entire commercial or five to ten minutes of Sesame Street begins to develop by about age three-and-a-half or four.

The nursery school teacher slowly attempts to get the child "desk-ready" by the end of the school year, while she comfortably accepts the wandering around, the curiosity, the spontaneous rebel expressions, the emotionality, and the rudimentary self control of the four- to five-year-old child. In kindergarten more will be expected from the five-year-old, namely: an ability to sustain attention, to control behavior, to control emotions, to control tone and pitch of voice and to control motor movements sufficiently to sit in the desk for reasonable periods of time (between thirty to sixty minutes at one time.) The capacity to follow instructions, to collaborate in play and work, to recognize and respect authority, to give appropriate verbal

12

responses, particularly in the appropriate expression of how he feels, are all part of the early socialization of the child.

For the truly hyperkinetic child, these social skills do not show progressive and predictable development. They may be irregular, patchy or totally absent, so that at seven he may not even be able to cope with the limits and requirements of a nursery school environment.

It must be remembered that formal schooling for large numbers of children is a relatively recent phenomena. The Greek root of the word "school" derives from "leisure time", namely leisure to pursue philosophy, discussion, and learning in the tradition of the men of classical Greece. Jesuit educators in the 17th century defined childhood as a time of innocence, during which the child should be protected from the corruption of adults, reared apart, and taught the word of the Lord. Private tutors and governesses became fashionable for aristocracy in the early 1600s, and slowly through the next century the middle classes began to aspire toward academic teaching for their children, too. It was after the French and Industrial Revolutions that the village schoolhouse grew to the proportions of a medium-sized school.

Previously, where children were part of a subsistance economy, of the daily household tasks, of earning a livelihood in factory work, there was no leisure to set aside in the pursuit of learning. Today legislation makes it mandatory that a child in the United States attend school until at least the age of sixteen. It is also mandatory in certain states that the child receive an education regardless of pathology: physical, social, intellectual, or psychological.

With increasing population, classes become larger. Conformity is expected, and there are between twenty and thirty children assigned to one classroom. With expanding knowledge, the curriculum becomes more demanding. Young people are expected to know a great deal more in order to exist competitively and comfortably in a complex urban society than they were a hundred years ago in a less mechanized world.

With expanding horizons, development of resources, affluence in an acquisitive, commercial society, not only have people acquired more material possessions, but also have purchased the capacity for far greater physical activity and expression than ever before. The range today of leisure and pleasure, of sports, activities and exercise, is vast. It is attractive and inviting. For many, active leisure pursuits counteract the sedentary requirements of job and mechanized transportation. In line with this, children's toys today also display the trend toward action and movement. Walking and talking dolls; mobile astronauts; mini-bikes and hotrods, all add to the action.

However, it must be stressed that, although this exercise may be regarded as "hyperactive", it is acceptable, productive activity where the participants, child or adult, sustain attention to complete the task or game. This differs from the hyperkinetic child or adolescent, whose activity is not productive, who does not sustain attention, nor complete a game or task. He is often too distractible to learn the desired activity.

Technology and sophistication add greatly to man's

capacity for speed and action. The Indianapolis 500, 1973, displayed participants able to cruise at 199 miles per hour. Supersonic jets and flights to the moon all contribute to the accelerated tempo characteristic of life in the 1970s. With better nutrition, and better control of infectious diseases, child development statistics show an accelerated rate of all of the growth milestones. Children are walking earlier, talking earlier, reading and writing earlier, menstruating an average of two years earlier than their 1850 counterparts.

The National Center for Health Statistics in 1971, accumulated data regarding infant development. Over 7,000 children between the ages of six and eleven were studied. Forty-eight percent of the children were reported as having started to walk unaided before the age of one, 95% walked by age 18 months, with girls walking earlier than boys. First real speech became apparent for nearly 43% of the children before age one, nearly 84% had spoken their first real word by 18 months. Again, here, the girls preceded the boys. Four percent of the children seemed slower than average in learning to do things by themselves. In this study, thumbsucking was reported in nearly all babies, but persistence after the age of six occurred in only 10%. Bedwetting after the age of four or five was reported in 15% of the children studied, with boys showing a higher incidence than girls.

After fifteen years of study on the East coast, psychiatrists Alexander Thomas and Stella Chess, of New York School of Medicine, and pediatrician Herbert Birch of Albert Einstein College of Medicine made some interesting

15

observations regarding babies, which they found were evident very early, before environment had had much effect. They described three types of temperament. (1) difficult infants (about 10%), (2) easy (the majority), (3) slow-to-warm-up babies.

The difficult infants were interesting in that they reacted extremely intensely to all stimuli; all responses were exaggerated. Instead of soft crying these would be howling, instead of quiet gurgling there would be uncontrolled laughter, which might end with a paroxysm of choking. Their schedules for eating and sleeping were irregular, with each change requiring long, difficult periods of adjustment. Since the investigators are still unsure of the exact origin, which on the surface would seem to be largely inborn, they emphasize that the difficult child needs to be understood early, so that parents may be reassured and not blame themselves for the difficult behavior. They should rather be comfortable in establishing a definite approach of limit-setting for the child, who might otherwise become a tyrant in the home as well as in later life. Gentle, but very firm and very consistent controls are essential for a child with a difficult temperament.

Easy children adapt rapidly, have regular habits, are happy in disposition, and usually fit in easily anywhere.

The slow-to-warm-up children are cautious and guarded, somewhat negativistic in mood, are inclined to withdraw from new situations, but with reassurance and encouragement, can be supported in their risk-taking and may eventually do satisfactory or even superior work.

The investigators stress that if these temperament

patterns are present from birth, parents and teachers could learn to handle the children effectively in most cases. Deep psychological disturbance may not necessarily underly the home or school difficulties of the difficult or slow-to-warm-up child. However, persistent difficulties of adjustment need to be considered individually. Timely and brief evaluation and intervention may be helpful in preventing maladjustment.

Some aspects of physical growth and development need to be understood. The rate of growth is extremely rapid in the first 18 months, and then somewhat slows until the age of five. The bones are not completely calcified, which accounts for the amazing number of falls without fractures sustained by infants and young children. Temporary teeth are present in a full set by the age of three. It is a good idea to start regular visits to the dentist by the age of three-and-a-half to prevent decay in these deciduous baby teeth. They should receive the same treatment as permanent teeth, since infection present for long periods in the mouth may be connected with generalized infection and impede good health of the growing child.

The large muscles develop, and together with them, skills in the use of arms, legs, and body. Various motor skills develop unevenly, and it is not unusual that the child loses interest in one newly-developed skill as he begins to acquire another. The child approaching five is extremely restless and energetic, he seems to need and want constant activity. Fatigue is never admitted. Parents who know the child will recognize that, although he denies being tired, his irritability, tendency to whine and cry, and to have temper tantrums, indicate that there is extreme fatigue in spite of the fact that he sets up a struggle to prevent going to bed. At such times of exhaustion, compassionate recognition of his valiant attempt to deny being tiny and tired, is more successful in coping with the situation than angry insistence by the parent that he *is* tired. A little extra attention and affection at this time, centered around some distraction, such as a warm bath with bubbles or plastic toys, can gradually undo the general tension in the home. This is frequently a time when many children invite and receive a spanking, which seems to relieve the friction, allow for tears and apologies, and finally restore quiet.

Round about the age of five the child is still extremely self-centered, shows a growing desire to make his own decisions, so that interference with his play or possessions is resented. The sense of property rights is much clearer regarding *mine* than thine! This is frequently difficult for adults to understand, since they already expect from the five-year-old the same set of values as they themselves have gradually developed through the years. Rudimentary child values will need repetitive, ongoing reinforcement on the part of *all* authorities. Significant adults in the home, as well as in the school setting, should repeatedly teach the child to respect the property of others as well as his own.

With increased social relationships, and a desire to make and keep friends, self-centeredness gradually becomes inhibited, and there is less grabbing pushing, and crying. He learns to collaborate with his peers. Although he may be verbally critical, he begins to share more, with or without protest.

Cooperative play with other children is greatly enjoyed. Some children will be shy, others will tend to show off and some will try to take over. Long-standing temperament patterns of the child need to be recognized, before adults become unduly concerned. At age 5 the interests for both boys and girls are similar. They play together comfortably, can recognize the skills of each other and compare their own skills, although they may episodically be quarrelsome.

A tendency to "romance" becomes clearly evident at this age, particularly when the children go to nursery school or kindergarten. A study by Broderick, in 1972, showed that children who boy–girl pair at age five tend to be more mature than five-year-olds who do not. The non-pairing children showed a tendency toward immaturity, whining and clinging to parents, and were slower to achieve the independence which is needed to form these romances. It was postulated that this type of relationship formed the nucleus of later heterosexual adjustment.

Play is usually vigorous in five-year-olds. They often manipulate each other, physically as well as verbally. Much imagination is evident, with laughter a frequent form of communication. Self-care is usually well-established by five. They are able to handle their toilet habits, getting a drink, etc., quite easily. The five-year-old who has poor speech or does not use speech readily for communication will have problems. He may be unable to achieve comfortable relationships with other

19

children. This may result in a pattern of withdrawal or of angry frustration with possible screaming tantrums.

Security within a family is a primary need. Where the family is unstable or fragmented, this security is threatened or absent. Companionship of peers, always important, may become truly critical to a lonely rejected child. Stable, concerned substitute parents in the form of neighbors or teachers may indeed rescue the developing child from emotional shipwreck by providing warmth and some basic need fulfillment.

A wide variety of activities to develop muscles seems to be intuitively devised by children. Climbing and hanging activities may terrify adults, but are well handled by the growing five-year-old. Moving toys such as cars, wagons, scooters, tricycles, and boats, may at first be frightening to a child, but as soon as the skill of manipulating the toy or the vehicle is mastered, there is great pleasure and repetitive enjoyment of the skill. Block-building, nail-pounding, mud and water play are all ancient forms of play which give delight to the growing child. Five is an age of great exploration of everything around the child. It is also a time of more detailed attention to his or her own body.

Discovery of the sex organs is extremely early, frequently at about age 18 months. The child finds that manipulation of the genitalia brings sensations which are enjoyable. Masturbation usually starts as early as one-and-a-half or two years. It may be noticed for the first time by parents at about the five-year age level. It is a completely normal developmental activity. Parents are assured that masturbation will *not* cause blindness, madness, mental deficiency, or deadly diseases. Some children will masturbate when they are in bed before going to sleep. Others will do so under stress. Mothers and teachers usually recognize that rocking may be a masturbatory equivalent and occur under similar conditions. Masturbation, rocking, and thumbsucking are all stimulations of self that bring solace and comfort to the child.

The element of relief of tension should be recognized and understood in order to avoid the panic some adults show on discovering masturbatory activity in the child. Curiosity regarding the bodies of other children is also common as the child grows and begins to socialize. This, too, is unremarkable and part of normal early psychosexual development.

As the body grows, so does vocabulary expand. Language then seems to increase logarithmically. Together with other new words, obscene or taboo words are learned. The child rapidly finds the "impact value" of these new and powerful words, which he brings home for trial on his family. He may be soundly spanked for his efforts. This usually serves to add greater angry impact to the specific words, which may then be recurrently used in times of intense anger. An alternative approach is to react matter-of-factly, expecting that these words will be included in the repertoire of the growing child. Ask the child if he or she understands the meaning of the new word. If not, give a brief definition, understandable to the child at whatever age. Volunteer that alternative, more

21

appropriate, accurate, and acceptable words may be used if one wishes to describe the specific activity. This is a most effective approach.

Parents should watch for an emergent pattern where a difficult five-year-old is constantly receiving negative attention. This may be in huge quantities due to persistent anger and conflict. It is sobering to reflect that it takes two to make a war, and if such provocative negative behavior is the style in the home over long periods, something should be done to alter the pattern. Change is more likely to come from a mature adult, who can elect to react in a different way. For one whole week the adult could with some difficulty and much self-control, ignore unacceptable behavior and respond positively only to acceptable behavior. This alteration of response often meets with dramatic and rapid improvement. It increases motivation toward better performance, and breaks the vicious circle of conflict between adult and child.

Up to the age of five, most children require about twelve hours of sleep. By the age of seven, usually this is lessened to about ten hours. Sleep difficulties are unusual in childhood. When they occur, the child needs to be studied and evaluated. Intense anxiety is usually the basis for night terrors, which are manifested by the child waking up and screaming. The majority of such episodes are transient, of brief duration, and obviously related to environmental stress. Brief intervention, involving both parents and child, is usually effective.

Some sleep disorders are less simple, and show different underlying dynamics. Intense separation anxiety may cause sleep refusal. After hearing parental fighting, or threats of mother stating she will pack her bags and leave, a three-year-old may cling and whine, or have temper tantrums and refuse to go to sleep, since his basic security is gravely threatened. If physical illness as a cause for sleep difficulties is excluded, then some emotional underlay is to be suspected and rapidly evaluated, since very few persons can withstand long periods of sleep deprivation. This is particularly true in the growing child. A "difficult child" as previously described, may show increased activity and reduced amounts of sleep from infancy, quite unrelated to any precipitant. He usually shows no resultant fatigue the following day, since it is his established physiological cycle, and rarely causes concern in his parents.

Occasionally hyperkinetic children may have sleep difficulties, which are usually more exaggerated than the variation noted in the "difficult child." The difficulty falling or staying asleep may finally bring the hyperkinetic child into an emergency room at 4:00 A.M. by exhausted parents. An acceptable sleep pattern can usually be established with satisfactory treatment.

Mealtimes, for most families with little ones, are usually mixtures of enjoyment and stress. Skill in self-feeding is gradually developed from an infantile tendency to use the whole hand to place everything in the mouth. Gradual skill is attained when the fingers can master a pincer grip, that is, using thumb and index finger to lift segments of food into the mouth. Skill in using a spoon, then a fork and knife, is slower in coming, as is the ability to drink from a glass, and to desist from screaming, spitting, missing the mouth and the plate, and messing the entire room. By five or six, mastery of eating skills has improved and the child can usually cope with lunchtimes at school. The "difficult child" may be excessively fussy about specific foods. The hyperkinetic child may be so distracted and attend so shortly to the task of eating, that the entire mealtime becomes a nightmare for all. The withdrawn child may be so preoccupied with internal thoughts and anxieties that he may not even be aware that the mealtime is in process around him, and need constant reminders to eat his food.

Normalcy has a wide range. Stresses may bring regressions even to a stable and mature person, regardless of age. Tiredness, hunger, separation or any unknown may represent more stress to the vulnerable child than the adult realizes. Endurance and previous experience form an important part of the acquired capacity to adapt to stresses. Having some knowledge of the possible duration of the stress is another essential component of an individual's coping devices. For example, a roadsign may indicate a restaurant in 10 miles. Father may have silently decided this will be their next stop to meet his needs for food and elimination, and mother may have recognized his alert recognition of the sign. Meanwhile to 5-year-old Tim, with a rudimentary sense of time, unable to read, with a full bladder, tired, hot and hungry, the stress seems endless and intolerable. He responds by irritable whimpering, demanding candy, restless stamping and finally wetting his pants, to everyone's final distress. Both parents may have been equally uncomfortable, however, they could endure their discomfort having done so many times before. Also, they knew relief was only about ten to fifteen minutes away; Tim did not. If his parents had been aware of his greater vulnerability, they could have assisted by asking how he felt; informing him that they planned to stop soon; comforting and distracting him by perhaps watching the speedometer and the roadsigns until the restaurant was reached; asking him to cross his legs and hold on, or making a stop sooner if he could not. They could thus have assisted the child back onto a path of healthy development.

I fain would fly
But that I fear to fall

Sir Walter Scott

3

The Hyperanxious Child

Perhaps most frequently mistaken for a Hyperkinetic child is a very anxious one, who certainly is hyperactive, but the activity has a very different expression from that seen in the hyperkinetic child. Not only is the underlying cause for the hyperactivity different, but its manifestation differs upon close study and observation.

The younger the child, the less verbal he will be. It is thus harder to recognize the feeling or emotion beneath observed behavior. Even many adults have difficulty identifying their own emotions. Usually they resist a pause in their daily activities to try to understand why they behave in one particular way rather than another.

For most people, anger is the emotion which they can most readily see and admit to. Anxiety is frequently neither recognized nor conceded, since it may for many have a connotation of "weakness". For other persons the op-

29

posite holds true. Anger may be so threatening, so poorly expressed and recognized, that their own feelings of underlying rage are totally denied. Their struggle to repress anger may at times result in conscious feelings of intense anxiety with an inability to deal with the underlying hostility.

Attitudes and approaches toward basic feelings are readily transmitted from adult to infant. A child's behavior is so bound up with the parents' response that family interactions inevitably develop. An example would be: an insecure young mother, somewhat afraid both of and for her first-born child, may be unable to leave the baby to cry himself to sleep. For reasons of her *own* anxiety, she may spend the night walking the floor, chastising her husband for not assisting her, trying to obtain his cooperation to do the same for the screaming infant. This usually results in two tired, anxious, somewhat angry people by morning. The interactions between this father and mother soon cease to be other than irritability and blame. The father may begin to view the child as the irritant. The mother may see herself as the only protector and ally of the infant. A coalition of mother and child then easily forms against the father. Thus, the infant, totally inadvertently, may become a wedge between the parents.

His role in his parents' conflict is usually clearly perceived by the child as he becomes a little older. With awareness of the power this gives him, he may even consciously play one parent against the other in his own interests, with resultant havoc in the home. However, the resultant parental battle creates anxiety in the child. A variety of possible emotions occur in the parents. In the resulting friction they may hurl accusations and threats toward each other, which are overheard by the child. Not infrequently threats of leaving each other are made, example: "You always protect the child, you don't listen to me, I don't rate in this house, I'm going to leave, and you two can make it on your own!" Threats may terrify the child and overwhelm him with guilt due to concern that he is indeed to blame for driving the parent away.

In fact, the conflict has occurred because of the immaturity of the couple, and their individual inability to share with a third person, their child. In trying to meet their own needs, they are unable to fulfill the needs of the child. Rivalry for the attention and affection of the child may supercede their role as caretaking parents.

In some instances a child may be receiving a quantitative excess of "love", but the *quality* may be pathological. Parents may explicitly or implicity demand a demonstrable return of love, or dependency and submission from child. This may cause conflict and anxiety, which may be more than the child can handle comfortably. Various symptoms may appear: agitation, whining, tantrums, tics, or phobias and withdrawal.

Although much has been written in recent years about the effects of one person upon another, there are large numbers of people who still insist that children of four or five are "too young to know", "too young to remember", "too young to feel anything". This is simply not so. Children, when asked to give a family history of their first memory, will surprise the psychiatrist by

31

seriously, carefully, and in detail, describe a memory from as early as the age of one-and-a-half, giving details of who was present, what happened, and how they felt. Children understand, feel, and remember, although they are not often requested to articulate their experiences.

The concept of "an emotionally disturbed child" is a controversial one. It implies that the emotional responses are *persistently* disturbed, or that the emotional difficulties developed as a response to overwhelming stress. While in some instances this may be true, in others the concept has yet to be proved. During the last fifty years parents of psychotic children have been harshly scrutinized and criticized as rejecting, cold, indifferent, and totally responsible for their children's desperate plight. Intensive study now seems to point in the direction of possible organic neurological factors or chemical causes in the child, with secondary emotional stresses as contributory in many psychotic children. With the severely disturbed child, the parents certainly may seem "different", but the examiner should question whether this is effect rather than cause? The behavior of the child is strange, unpredictable, and frequently un-understandable even to trained professionals. The parents may feel helpless and hopeless. They may possibly be afraid of their psychotic child's behavior.

It must be remembered that there is no specific training for parents to be parents. For the most part, each parent has been exposed to the parenting of his own specific parents, where the quality may have been good, bad, or indifferent. Each parent may elect to repeat the exact pattern of their own rearing, or do the very opposite, if they have personally felt pain in such rearing. When two persons are brought together in marriage, their individual plans for rearing their own children may be agreeably collaborative. However, their goals and attitudes may be completely conflictual and cause a great deal of interpersonal friction. In their struggle the child may be manipulated into an alliance with one parent and hostility against the other. The interaction becomes destructive to all, particularly to the most vulnerable—usually the child.

Sometimes even the most stable and well-meaning parents are unable to cope with one particular child, and know it. They are not helped by being made to feel guilty by professionals. It would be more beneficial to interpret the patterns of exchange so that parents can undo self-defeating but recurrent interactions that unwittingly cause disturbance to the child.

Many times pathological interaction is totally *un*conscious, although repetitive. Only when the actions are brought to full consciousness can the parents become aware of them and then do something to alter the pattern. Most parents in a helping situation show a capacity to grow and become more mature. Although they frequently slip back into old patterns, many show a willingness to change. Helping personnel usually understand, and even anticipate such difficulties. It is not easy to change old or fixed behavior, but with goodwill and effort, it is possible.

In the newborn baby, physical discomfort should be differentiated from emotional discomfort. Sensations giving pain, such as skin conditions and abrasions, are more clearly recognized since they can be externally observed. However, when the pain is internal, from distension or spasm of the gut, it is much more difficult for the parents to recognize. The mother may presume that, since there is no visible external cause for pain, the cause is internal. Pain and discomfort may cause the same kind of crying in the infant. Hunger and elimination are recurrent needs in the baby.

A father in the first month of having his first twin children described the babies as "a noise at one end and a mess at the other." The task of consistently taking care of infant needs may be an exhausting one to parents. They may never have been faced with such demanding, *repetitive*, and mundane tasks. In the whole glow and glamor of "becoming a parent", one or both of the couple may not have taken into account the ongoing, everyday, exhausting aspects of infant care. A sudden realization may come within the first few months of "being cooped up in the house." The couple may previously have been active socially and in sports and now find themselves bound down. They also might be trying to be "perfect" parents, or feel guilty about leaving the child with sitters. They may also suddenly be strapped financially by having one less salary and the expense of meeting the baby's needs.

Resentment toward the infant not uncommonly occurs, as parents blame the infant for changes in their lifestyle. They resolve this in their adaptation to being parents. Some realize that having a child is their own need —to create another self or to obey religious rules. Some freely acknowledge yet other needs, such as for activity, for social life, and these parents comfortably arrange to separate from the infant on occasion.

The mother will already have realized that short separations from the infant during the day may cause howls of protest, which she and the infant must endure, as she gets her work done. However, some mothers may not be able to tolerate a crying baby. A state of symbiosis may result where the mother has the child constantly with her during waking periods, fostering in both self and baby a fantasy of total oneness which becomes increasingly difficult to undo. Such a mother needs reassurance that it is both right and necessary for the child to sustain multiple small separations in the interest of his own independent development.

The child's beginning boundaries of self become defined in his separations from mother. The infant must learn that mother is not at the end of every cry. This happens when each scream does not predictably bring the magical appearance of mother at the side of the crib. Magical thinking is part of the inner world of the child, and persists for some time as the child begins to learn that thinking and wishing do not create reality. It is an early learning experience to tolerate the anxiety of separation. At first this is for short periods of time, which gradually increase with age, until the child can separate for some hours with sitters, for nursery school, for grade school, for longer periods of time, at camp, then college, and finally the total separation in adulthood.

Separation brings anxiety and depression at *any* age. Excellent studies on very young infants reveal that the crying of infants under six months usually relates to physical needs, but from the age of six months, prolonged separation from the mother can bring intense emotions recognizable as anxiety. John Bowlby of the Tavistock Clinic, London, described a sequence of behavior which commonly occured when children between the ages of six months and four years were removed from their mother to whom they were attached, and given to the care of strangers for prolonged (over 6 month) periods. Three main phases were noted: (1) protest (2) despair (3) detachment. The protest phase is clearly observed to be related to separation and the anxiety of such separation. It is an active struggle to restore the threatened relationship by protesting (namely screaming) and by difficult behavior, tantrums, struggling, and trying to run and find the mother. The second phase is despair expressed as grieving and mourning for the lost mother. This may be expressed openly as tears, crying, whining, and whimpering, or quietly by a sad expression, by the refusal to eat, by difficulties with sleeping. The child may lie and stare and be unable to fall asleep or wake repeatedly during the night. Detachment or withdrawal is a defense, finally, against feelings of anxiety or depression. The child becomes poorly responsive to others, and will not relate well. He is seemingly reluctant to trust and come close, for fear of being hurt in the same way again. He may not understand whether the current relationships are to be permanent or not.

The child of six may sometimes be fidgety, tense and overactive in the classroom. This behavior may nonverbally express for him a great deal of anxiety about repeated separation each morning from his mother, particularly where there is a basic fear that she will not be there on his return to the home. There may be apprehension or even real fear of injury to the mother, particularly if there have been physical fights the day before. Perhaps an alcoholic father may have threatened or beaten the mother or there may have been threats of divorce and leaving by one or the other parent. This may be totally unknown to the teacher who struggles to make the child conform and sit in the desk. Sometimes such a child will settle down if the anxiety is moderate. The teacher may sometimes be reassuring or the schoolwork may prove engaging enough to distract the child from his inner anxiety. The fact that a child is able to sit still when interested; to concentrate when involved with a specific task; to complete it without being excessively distracted, is an important clue that the episodes of fidgeting and preoccupation do *not* indicate a true "Hyperkinetic child", who is driven by an internal dynamo of excessive stimulation from the brain to the muscles, precluding any voluntary control by the child.

Management

The overanxious child responds to concern and reassurance from the teacher, from the parents, from interested adults. However, to be effective for longer periods, such reassurance needs to be *informed*, namely, related to the actual perceived cause of the anxiety, such as, "Mother will be at home, and safe, when you get back", if the teacher is aware that this is one of the basic anxieties. Sometimes, it is of great benefit to allow a very anxious

37

child to make a phone call to his mother to make sure she is safe and at home. The teacher could explain to mother why they are calling before putting the child on the line. Firstly, the exchange tells the child that someone understands his anxiety. Secondly, the call emphasizes that all is well for that time period at least. The teacher should realize that the stress regarding separation from parents may be recurrent and repeated each day for a specific child. If the problem at home is a chronic one, namely, ongoing home conflict with severe marital maladjustment, then active therapeutic intervention may be essential at a family level.

The overanxious child who brings his trouble to school with him is unable to leave it at home. Not uncommonly, one sees children of varying ages handling the same stress in different ways. From the same home, an 11-year-old may be coping extremely well by competing in sports, doing well in the classroom, finding interesting activity and satisfaction for himself outside of the home, for he is beginning to separate successfully. However, his six-year-old brother may be whiny and irritable, settling down with his regular trusted teacher, yet impossible when there is a substitute teacher. This is because separation from his regular teacher may recreate for him the pain of separating from his mother.

The behavior related to anxiety may show a wide range. In addition to clinging, crying and withdrawal, there may be temper tantrums, running out of the classroom, or disruptive behavior which then labels the child as "bad" and often sends him to the principal, compounding the difficulties. The teacher, often unaware of any underlying anxiety, may finally request referral for professional help, saying the child is "hyperactive".

The large majority of mildly anxious children are handled not by medication, but by understanding some of the underlying causes, then working to change those causative factors that are amenable to change. Reassuring the child when reassurance is possible, finding alternative means of gratification for a specific child, and assisting growth toward a mature ability to separate, when necessary, from the significant persons in the child's life, are all important. It is to be stressed again that there is a wide variation in the range of normal. The shy, cautious child is not necessarily highly abnormal. With extra time and encouragement, he can learn to live with a low level of anxiety, perhaps just a little higher than the normal anxiety endured by most of the human race.

Where the anxiety is uncomfortable and present over long periods of time (for a child this would mean for weeks and months) referral of the family for evaluation and treatment is of long range importance, to prevent unhealthy, persistent habit patterns. Very rarely does a child show symptoms without there being causal or resultant problems in other members in the family. Referral may then be therapeutic not only for the anxious child, but for others members too. This is good health care, preventing more serious problems later.

The Psychotic Child

When the anxiety is severe or sustained it may be disintegrative, causing panic or agitation. The panic may result in episodes of bizarre behavior. There may in certain cases be an organic basis for unusual behavior. Congenital abnormalities affecting the brain, the intellect, and the general level of functioning may result in the person being recognized from childhood as mentally retarded. Such persons may show disruptive, bizarre behavior, which may include features of intense, explosive motor activity, screaming, self-mutilation, biting or hitting themselves, headbanging, tearing off their clothes, intense rocking, open masturbation. Usually such behavior, with or without accompanying mental retardation, is recognized and described as psychotic, since it is felt that the child, adolescent, or adult cannot conform to or be brought back into contact with the demands of reality.

Psychotics' behavior may endanger family, peers, or teachers. Even parents may be at risk when they are unable to control the threatening behavior. Such persons are usually easily identified as needing professional help, and taken to emergency rooms for medical assistance. Sometimes a clear precipitating cause is evident. However, in many instances the anxiety seems to be related to internal rather than external stimuli. Frequently, there is a combination of both internal and external factors.

It is to be emphasized that psychosis is not necessarily a permanent condition. There may be fluctuations, with or without medication. These fluctuations may occur within the same hour, as the person slips in and out of psychosis, or shows periods of disturbed behavior for many days, then remissions for many weeks or months. Sometimes the psychosis may be related to simple causes such as a toxin or a severe infectious disease, which may subside. Toxins of ingested drugs—whether accidental or deliberate, prescribed or abused—usually are excreted by the body after a period of time (days to weeks.) Certain children with psychotic behavior, however, present a permanent inability to meet lifes' demands. Some psychoses can appear without underlying physical or organic cause being revealed on medical investigation.

Management

Whether the cause is defined or not, most psychoses today respond to specific medications. Both parents and physicians should be flexible yet careful in their search for a suitable drug for a particular child. Reactions are highly individual. There is a wide range of available similar medications. Frequently it is only by trial and error that the optimum drug is found to restore a child to previous good functioning. Medication provides a chemical internal control for the intensely disturbed child. Usually small doses of phenothiazine tranquillizers are most effective.

Day care centers, behavioral modification approaches, special education classrooms today all offer alternative outpatient therapeutic options to the solitary approach of permanent hospitalization offered prior to the 1970s.

The road is long and very lonely for the psychotic child. It is extremely rough and strewn with boulders for the despairing family. It is bitter and angry for the denying or rejecting family who cannot understand or cope with their burden. They hurl blame at each other, at the child, at every professional who fails to provide the desperately desired cure.

The family of the psychotic child needs very special understanding, supportive, long-term, (not necessarily intensive) follow-up, preferably family therapy, so that all members may express themselves and share their task of assisting the troubled member.

It is not always easy to say the right thing at the right time, but it is far more difficult to leave unsaid the wrong thing at the tempting moment.

Benjamin Franklin

4

The Hyperaggressive Child

For the concerned adult, parent or teacher, dealing with the angry, rebellious, aggressive child, the tempting moment is frequent and recurrent. The tendency to lose control of one's composure and respond emotionally to the child's aggression with immediate counter-aggression, verbal or physical, is indeed tempting. Coping with the child requires from the adult: awareness, self control and composure, together with a real understanding that this is the child's way of trying to express many other emotions, while on the surface he shows only the irritating and provocative behavior.

It is important for parents and other adults concerned with children to recognize the rhythms of growth, the fluctuations between expansive and quiet ages, and between harmonious periods. Calm is often followed by turmoil, and vice-versa, with no child fitting into exactly the same mold as another at the same age. Individual variation is wide. As the child passes through different stages, there are positive and negative features of each. A child may be labelled "bad" or "terrible" so repetitively and consistently during a phase that the child's basic self-esteem suffers.

A four-year-old may often seem overbold as he struggles to establish self-confidence and an independence which he lacked a few months previously. Similarly, a six-year-old may be rebellious, aggressive, demanding, and selfish; he may hate one moment and love the other, but at other times he can show tremendous enthusiasm and excitement for life. This boisterousness may be followed at age seven with a time of unhappiness, whining, and moodiness, which seems to be a complete reversal after the preceding hectic year. Parents may find with surprise that they now need to urge this same child to go out and play.

It is to be remembered that all social beings exhibit a process of socialization which can be divided into two parts: *primary socialization*, which usually takes place in early childhood, and *secondary socialization*, which occurs later in life, as in the formation of career and sexual relationships.

Primary socialization usually influences the kind of secondary socialization which will take place. Both are learned phenomena. Clinical evidence in man and experimental work with animals demonstrate that once learned, primary socialization patterns are rarely unlearned. If critical periods have passed without the child having learned primary socialization, such patterns are very difficult to learn when older, and to adopt later as an integral part of self. This is particularly true of patterns of aggressive expression which have been uninhibited. In many cultures, by taboo, primary socialization inhibits free or public expression of instinctual drives of sex and aggression. Some societies socialize by language taboos. Each culture teaches the child generally acceptable modes of expression in the interest of group living and general order.

Early experiences are permanently, although not necessarily irreversibly, retained. When the capacity to learn emerges, the child perceives the environment, differentiates objects, and associates a specific person such as mother with gratification of needs and alleviation of discomforts. The permanence and consistency of this relationship, and the continued, repetitive seeking of further contact with this loved person, who pleasurably meets needs and alleviates discomfort, institutes the phenomena which is called positive reinforcement in experimental psychology. This reinforcement should predictably give pleasure and/or avoid discomfort. Due to repetition, a habit pattern forms. Thus, if the child is reared with a mother-figure who is associated with pleasant experiences, a pattern of thinking develops which is secure, trusting and lasting.

Overindulgence creates problems, particularly where a parent, fearing loss of love of the child, fails to provide primary socialization. This should provide external controls by adult authority, from which internal self-controls should gradually be learned by the growing child. Self-control or discipline in the early years is learned in the context of parent love. The child conforms so as not to lose love and approval. Children can thus be patterned into behavior which is pleasing and acceptable to the loved parents or teachers (parent substitutes). If there is insufficient or inconsistent parental love, or if the parents reject the child, primary socialization is rudimentary or deficient, causing conflict, chronic aggression, anger, self-rejection, poor self-esteem, maladjustment, and explosive behavior. The child who needs the attention of the loved parent will then substitute obtaining of negative attention for positive. Instead of love and tenderness, he might recurrently provoke an angry spanking. At that moment the child is fully aware that the attention of the parent is 100% *his*, even though it is physically painful.

All humans live with daily irritants, to which they respond with anger. Outbursts are usually transient, and everyone in the home can usually comfortably endure such occasional episodes. It is the chronic, repetitive on-going day-to-day angry conflict, aggression and counter-aggression; or the unpredictable, unjustified attacks, that will breed the hyperaggressive child.

In many an instance, the parent will insist that the child is well-behaved at home, while school authorities describe impossible behavior on the bus and disruptive behavior in the classroom, with constant fights and suspensions. For the child, the story may be that due to fear of intense retaliatory physical beatings he manages to control his aggression within range of his parents. The underlying dynamic of the explosive behavior away from home is that the pressure of the anger builds up to a point of explosive eruption as soon as he leaves home. For him the threat of loss of love of teacher, principal and bus driver is less than is loss of parental love. He is angry yet emotionally bound with his parents.

The exact age at which experience exerts maximum effect on the growing personality is a fundamental, but extremely complex, question, not given to simple answers. A widely accepted generalization, from intense longitudinal observation of children and families, from study of animal behavior, from clinical psychology, from learning theory, is that early habits are extremely persistent. They sometimes prevent the formation of new habits, and early perceptions deeply affect future learning. Childhood social contacts definitely determine the character of adult social behavior.

These facts are widely known, but also discounted by many parents who bring a child in for psychiatric evaluation, insisting that the home is stable, while the child gives a history of early memories of intense conflict, physical fighting, terror that his father would kill his mother in their battles, and finally divorce and a later remarriage. The mother is usually surprised to hear that all these details are remembered by the child. "He was too young to remember", "He was three when we divorced." Yet the child, now eight, can describe the behavior, size and looks of the absent father.

Some children will block out or deny any early memories. Sometimes this is an unconscious defense, at times the denial is a deliberate guardedness. The child may fear retaliation from the now only available parent. There looms possible loss of love or even separation if he "betrays" information, which he knows may upset his mother. The child may feel none of the anger felt by the mother toward the divorced father, may indeed identify with him, and some of the child's explosive behavior may simply be an imitative attempt to "be as strong as he was."

Current rivalries may create intense anger and anxiety in the child. A new baby from the new father may be taking mother completely away from the older child, who is now labeled as "the bad one." He may become the scapegoat, and receive only negative attention, which he may in fantasy blame upon the arrival of a new baby sister. Every girl in the bus and classroom then becomes a good target for his anger as he vicariously aggresses the baby sister.

In a similar way, anger which he may not express toward his mother may be expressed toward a female teacher or aide. This may relieve some of his pent-up negative feelings toward the mother whom he both loves and hates. There may be an additional factor of repeating a habit pattern of seeking negative attention in the schoolroom. If the latter is the case, simple reassurance and follow-through by parent or teacher that good behavior as well as bad will receive attention often successfully subsides the explosions.

Exceptions will occur. There may be a truly unconscious buildup of anxiety, depression, and rage, where the child will be internally driven to explode in order to handle his internal pain. This type of hyperaggressive child, not uncommonly, is referred by teachers to psychiatrists as "hyperactive", "disruptive", "impossible to manage," "underachieving". The child is sending out signals that he is still struggling to cope with a very unhappy situation, and indeed, although his behavior is difficult for others around him, it is more wholesome for the child himself, since he is still making some attempt to cope with and adjust to life, unfair as he perceives it.

The child who instead of "acting-out" withdraws recurrently into his own fantasy life, where his rage can be worked out in imagination, is of far graver concern to the psychiatrist. This withdrawal means, in a sense, that the child has given up hope that powerful adults of any kind will pick up his messages, and bring him help.

The capacity to articulate is still rudimentary in a child. Often professional assistance is needed before the child's verbalization of his true feelings becomes possible. It will take time, also tolerance of silences and of "I don't know" from the child. Gradually after a few visits, strangeness decreases, while trust increases. The child will then rewardingly open up.

In evaluating the hyperaggressive child it is crucial that the evaluation include *both* parents. If their history excludes the possibility that this child has a lifelong personality type of a more assertive, always "difficult child" as described in previous chapters, but includes intense and persistent aggressiveness, the parents should be carefully questioned for possible antecedent causes for hostility. These need to be understood and corrected. Exact details of the early history are important, when and how

51

frequently aggressive behavior was observed, how it was handled early and currently. Were there periods where the aggressive behavior was allowed uninhibited expression and was there actual pleasure or gratification on the part of one or both parents when early aggressive behavior was witnessed? If so, then pleasing of the parents could have been built into the child's particular behavior pattern. In many instances, passive parents vicariously act out their own aggressive impulses through the behavior of the child.

It is not infrequent that parents will describe with some regret how their child "unfortunately" got caught in a stealing episode. This clearly indicates the degree of sanction that is given in the home to such unacceptable behavior. The parents insist that they never verbalize approval of stealing but always tell the child to be "good, honest, law-abiding", yet values are transmitted by more than their words in the home. When articles shoplifted by a child are found but not returned by the parents to the store-owner, the child learns the double message: while he may receive some small token punishment, the parents are not averse to retaining and using the stolen goods. Likewise, a child might be encouraged to "go out and beat him up," giving pleasure to the parents when he does. However, if the same act comes to the attention of the principal, the reprimanded parents may reverse their reaction, and punish him. This confuses the child.

Violence, either verbal or physical, between parents or child and parent, or between significant others within the home situation, is a crucial mode of learned behavior.

The child himself will later react similarly to perceived stress of any kind. Inconsistency in upbringing or parental rejection promote insecurities. The child never knows what to expect.

"Fight and flight" are normal counterparts of self-preservatory reflexes in every living organism. Where uncontrolled and unpredictable hostility is prevalent in the home, the child may feel trapped, helpless, defenseless, chronically fearful, and act out his own counter-aggression toward younger sibs, peers and society. This child struggles aggressively to manipulate his environment, denies the need for affection, and is negativistic and resentful when made to feel helpless in his repetitive clash with authority.

If these experiences are persistently present over a period of years, and no corrective emotional experiences are obtained before adolescence, the nucleus is formed for the young delinquent, for personality disorders. and for poor general adjustment as adults. They remain unable to control and cope with their own emotions of aggression.

Management

Therapy is essentially directed toward the *entire* family, aiming to correct the interactions that promote the aggressive behavior. In some cases, therapy may be long and difficult, since there must first be an understanding of, sometimes a modification of the value system of the parents. They will need support, confrontation and encouragement. Sometimes medication for the child or parents is useful to change old patterns of irritability or explosiveness. The child may then receive more recognition which helps toward his changing in a way that can give the whole family alternative ways of interacting.

A "behavior modification" approach can be most effective. By observing recurrent unacceptable patterns, the stimulus (S) from the child and usual response (R) from parents can be identified. In the S-R interaction, change needs to be achieved and maintained. It is most logical to start with changing the adult response. Example: at mealtimes, "Food Refusal (S)——Angry Battle" (R) becomes "Food Refusal (S)——Non-Battle (R2)" (the plate is silently removed and covered.) Other food should *not* be given at this time. Later demands for food should be met by quietly presenting the original plate. The message is clear and quickly learned. This conditioning method may be called "extinction" (of an unacceptable pattern) or "negative reinforcement" (resultant hunger.) It works. It can be applied in dozens of ways.

The author's observation is simply that it takes *two* to make a war. If the parent does not engage in primitive aggression at the child's level, the child learns more mature ways of control.

Further application of current research into learning theory and behavior modification techniques is discussed at some length in the following chapter.

These things shall be!
A loftier race than e're the
world hath known shall rise,
with flame of freedom in
their souls, and light of
knowledge in their eyes.

John Addington

5

Discipline

The concept of discipline has been misunderstood and misused for centuries. Discipline is essential to child-rearing, education, survival and productivity. An entire chapter is devoted here to its study and exposition.

Discipline in the 1960's was a dirty word. It had become synonymous with harshness, repression, oppression and cruelty. In the restrictive Victorian era, when children were to be seen and not heard, discipline had come to mean threats, punishment, fear, rigid authority, holding onto irrational rules, and also righteous anger. A much cited proverb was: "Spare the rod and spoil the child," implying that utilizing harsh methods was essential to prevent destructive development in the growing child.

A tenacious theory for ages held that a child's will should necessarily be "broken" before he could accept or follow directions. This stems from Ecclesiasticus in the Apocrypha:

> Bow down his neck while he is young
> and beat his sides while he is a child:
> lest he grow stubborn and regard thee not,
> and so be a sorrow of heart to thee.

Paradoxically many choose to disregard a sage observation from Proverbs 26:21:

> As coals are to burning coals and wood to fire, so
> an angry man stirreth up strife.

This latter response of counter-aggression is very pertinent to childrearing and was explored at some length in the previous chapter.

Parents reared in fundamentalist doctrines may, in the complex 20th century, be sincerely following ancient childrearing laws of the Old Testament.

It takes courage, maturity and flexibility to change and explore new ways of understanding and interpreting human behavior. Intellectual honesty and parental concern usually combine to meet the present needs of the troubled child and family.

Sigmund Freud, Viennese born physician, was himself reared in the repressive social structure he later explored and criticized. In *Civilization and its Discontents* (1930), he outlined how neuroses resulted from society's inhibition of an individual's instincts in the interest of community living. The impact of Freud's theories was world-wide, having particular influence in education and on educated parents, who were most careful to avoid "traumatizing" their children. A "permissive period" ensued from the 1940s to the late 1960s, interpreting Freud's exposition of unconscious motivation as behavioural "determinism." Expression rather than suppression of impulses was considered a new freedom.

The vivid World War II view of brainwashing of children and individuals, and imprisonment of large masses of people by police states, and militarism in all its variations had, in addition, provided dramatic distaste for forceful repression. The inevitable aftermath of wartime "indoctrination" was human agony, indignity and violation. In the United States, a general trend developed. Recognition of the individual was emphasized, with strong reactions against anything resembling "socialism," "suppression," or "Communism".

The last ten years have shown a tendency to escalate movements for civil rights: recognition of minority groups, women's liberation, protection of the environment, and assertion of individuality. However, together with a slow evolution of "freedom" and "liberation" from many attitudinal chains, we have also reaped "freedom" and "liberation" from rules and from orderly conduct. A decade of riots, rebellions, and hot summers, has necessitated a closer look at laissez-faire leadership, in contrast with authoritarian leadership through firm, clear and defined rules and laws.

Many are taking a new look at discipline, in an attempt to study and understand its underlying mechanisms and dynamics. The Latin roots of the word discipline are interesting; it means "to take apart or to hold apart." Among the many definitions given in Webster's are: instruct, educate, train, regulate, correct, chastize and punish. Another meaning reads: "acceptance of rules and methods as in a specific discipline such as mathematics, law, medicine."

In common everyday usage the word discipline has come to mean training in self-control and orderly conduct. It is thus artificial to separate discipline from learning, which is based on control of thoughts, memory, visual and graphic perceptions, hearing, body and behavior.

Two types of discipline are recognized: negative discipline through fear of punishment, and positive discipline through pleasurable or positive identification with others, or with a specific philosophy or task. Negative and positive disciplines may superficially be equally efficient, but the former has to be maintained by strict surveillance and by constant threat of consequences, whereas the latter is self-sustaining and usually much longer–lasting.

Using a rigid discipline of methods and rules, man has gone back to relearn behavior in experimental laboratories. Behavioral scientists have literally taken apart isolated actions in order to study the immensely complex field of learning.

Learning Theory

Learning theory has greatly contributed to our current understanding of how we learn behavior control, which is the capacity to internalize outside controls by developing self-control. Example: To avoid the pain of being yelled at by parent, motorist or crossing–guard, a child learns to control his impulse to dash across a busy road. He tells himself internally to stop, and in this way he pleases authority. Additionally there is high survival value for himself. This self-control is also part of primary socialization.

In the whole process of development from the primitive infant to the sophisticated adult, control of appetites is imperative. Essential drives of aggression, sex and dependency must be mastered in some way. This is achieved by a process of socialization which is the deliberate, repetitive curbing of impulsive individual expression, in the interests of harmonious group living and overall survival. Toilet-training is socialization, as is any form of collaborative work, study or play.

The developmental stages from infant to adult display a full range from total self–centeredness of the newborn, to a capacity for sharing. Willingness to care for and meet the needs of others occurs only with the advent of maturity. From "me" to "thee" is the progression, and it is a slow one. Without maturity it may not be successfully attained.

Cellular growth has a magnificient innate discipline. There is a specific order and predictable stages, from the simple, single living cells into complex systems, which each perform specific functions but all collaborate with each other in a unified whole, comprising the human being. In a similar way both intellect (learning) and emotion (feeling) develop from the simple and undifferentiated into the complex, elaborate totality of human mind and feeling. The knowledge of human development is important in understanding what is expectable behavior from children at various stages of growth.

To teach, to learn and to discipline self or others are similar. The words are often used synonomously. Studying learning is at the same time a study of discipline and therefore of the teaching process.

Useful contributions from learning theory laboratories are:

1. that the child must have the capacity to perform or learn the task which is being taught. Example: the neurogical pathways in a 6-month-old are not yet developed enough for the child to learn to run.

2. that certain conditions are necessary for the process of learning, such as alertness and freedom from excess anxiety.

3. that distraction experimentally, in both human and animal subjects, obliterates any electroencephalic record of verbal stimuli from the relevant auditory area of the brain. In everyday situations this means that an attempt to make a point, give instructions, or rebuke a child who is distracted by a temper tantrum or by extreme fear, is a total waste of time for the parent or teacher. The child has to be attentive in order to learn or even to hear.

4. that learning by punishment is a *temporary* suppressant and does not eliminate undesirable behavior. Constant negative reinforcement is necessary.

62

5. that positive re-inforcement of acceptable behavior is more long-lasting, and can then be widely spaced so that finally the task itself becomes pleasurable and its own positive reward.

6. that extinction techniques have been most successful experimentally both with human and animal subjects. These consist of totally ignoring unacceptable behavior while generously recognizing and rewarding acceptable behavior.

7. that after the age of 12 months it is necessary for all children to sustain the multiple small anxieties due to short separations from mother. This enhances development of individuation. Boundaries of self as separate from mother have to be learned. Independence to develop begins with the child's capacity to tolerate this "normal" anxiety.

Self-discipline begins in infancy, the moment an infant first begins, at a few weeks or months of age, to tug away from his feeding bottle. It may be messier for the child to feed himself; more untidy for him to dress himself; less clean when he attempts to bathe himself; less perfect for him to comb his own hair; but unless his mother learns to sit on her hands and allow the child to cry and to try, she will overdo for the child, and independence will be delayed.

From doing-for-self comes a strong sense of self and self-satisfaction, and self-esteem. Control of drives is

63

learned by either identifying with the adult (to please and obtain praise) or behaving in a certain way to avoid unpleasant consequences. Mastery represents a new capacity in the child to internalize rules, which then can be followed spontaneously without needing constant external supervision or punishment.

It is a wise parent who allows the child to learn the full natural consequences of every action, within the limits of safety. A child who misses the bus and walks to school, comes late and takes the full natural consequences of his tardiness, eventually learns the discipline of getting up on time in order to avoid the undesirable consequences of being late. The parent who rushes the late child to school deprives him of his learning experience. The home, with its small daily tasks and exchanges, is a stage which is representative of the arena of later life. The child who is constantly protected from experiencing the consequences of his own behavior by an indulgent parent is ill-equipped to meet the harsh realities of later adult life, where there will be no doting mother to chauffeur him through the competitive realities of the complex life of the 1970s.

Much of behavior in day-to-day life is modified by negative unpleasurable responses, which are definable as punishment. Punishment is anything that gives pain to the total person. Since pain responses (physically or psychologically) vary with individuals, the definition of what is punishment becomes much broadened.

A registered nurse who had been trained in psychiatry came in for an emergency consultation. She felt overwhelmed and unable to cope with her four-year-old, whose growing independence was a challenge. The mother stated emphatically, "I don't believe in spanking children." She was attempting to control her first-born by long explanatory lectures of why the girl's behavior was wrong. She then made the child sit on the stairs silently for an hour at a time, out of sight of the room in which she herself was working.

It came as a rude shock to her when she was asked whether she was using verbal and emotional spankings instead? For an active four-year-old to endure the prolonged social isolation of not being allowed to see the mother, as well as the prolonged physical inactivity, was far more harsh and less effective than more appropriate immediate, mild physical discipline. An interesting sociological finding in the 1970s is that educated, upper-class mothers tend to avoid physical punishment, which is used more frequently lower down the social scale.

It is good judgment to make penalties and controls as relevant to unacceptable behavior as is possible. *Example*: a young child who has stayed away for many hours later than the home rules allow, could be deprived of use of the bicycle, upon which he left the home, for a day or two. Where money is being taken without permission, repayment should be requested, and purse and change should be locked away. Consistency is also important in that the child should be able to predict the consequences of certain behaviors. This realization of the consequences gives him some choice in testing his independence and in paying the price for what he begins to consider an important enough value or privilege.

The Hyperactive Child

The younger the child, the more immediate the disciplinary consequences should be, since the capacity to remember and make the association is still only rudimentary in the young child. He will not remember five hours or five days later the unacceptable behavior for which he is then being punished.

Punishment is a necessary reality of life; whether we euphemize by calling it "negative reinforcement" or "the consequences of unacceptable behavior", the end result is pain to the person. The small hand-spank for a child has its analogue in the adult world—traffic violation fines; loss of pay for those days adults do not work. There are many non-verbal forms of punishment, such as a look, an expression, silence, avoidance, a turned back, a threatening raise of arm, fly-swatter or wooden spoon. These all rapidly become indicators of disapproval within a particular situation or home.

Important to realize, however, is that repeated, relentless use of shame and blame can devastate the self-esteem of child as well as of adult. It is crucial that parents watch what they say. Other children in the home rapidly note accusatory tendencies. Very soon one child will be selected as the family scapegoat. To avoid such shame/blame techniques, adults should clearly differentiate *person* and *behavior, example*: "I like you, but not your dragging mud into the house." Criticize the unacceptable behavior but avoid name-calling. Attempt to elevate the child's behavior to more mature awareness and effort, rather than depreciate him personally.

Pleasurable responses also have many non-verbal

components; a smile; a wink; a pat on the back; ruffling the hair; a hug and a kiss, all convey recognition and approval. More concrete evidence are the stars, checkmarks, the happy faces used in the classroom; good report cards; rewards or gifts or candy. For adults it is the monthly paycheck.

The smile is perhaps the most important form of pleasant human exchange and reward given from person to person. It has great value from mother to infant; from adult to child; from child to child; from adult to adult. Most children will do more in response to such recognition than they will to avoid a frown. Exploitation of the smile in the 1970s reached major proportions in the United States, when millions of smiling faces were sold on pillows and pajamas; dishes and dresses. However, the highest value of a smile is still on the human face, and deprivation of parental smiles may indeed have long-lasting effects on a child, since both love and laughter are learned in the very early years in the home.

There are other deprivations which act as punishment, namely social isolation, such as sending the child to a room which removes him from the persons of parent, siblings or other friends. Such separation may be endured with pain, anger or anxiety by the child. Thus, this unpleasant consequence of unacceptable behavior may be a positive learning experience if a child is ready for such learning in age and understanding, and if he feels it is merited. However, if the child is too young, or lacks intellectual capacity or is unjustly isolated, the deprivation may serve to act as an *un*-understandable stress to such a

67

child, and may provoke pain and retaliatory counter-aggression. There is fine line between what is beneficial and what is harmful. Evaluation and judgment are required each time before utilizing punishment of any type.

Outer controls and limits are provided for the growing child when those around him give clear repeated verbal indications of what he may or may not do. Setting up clear limits in the home environment is sometimes done without clearly verbalizing these for the child. There may be an expectation that the child will automatically become aware of the limits, abide by them, and not require anyone to outline them. A common example might be the fact that the family room is an acceptable play area for the child, whereas his parents' bedroom is not; that the Kool-Aid is within his limits to use whereas father's beer is not. The more clearly the parents outline such limits the fewer problems there will be. Gradually direct external supervision will no longer be necessary as the child learns internally what is permitted and what is not, and then is able to control himself without the essential presence of an authority.

Disruptive behavior commonly affords a ready indicator of poorly controlled emotions, particularly if the reaction is prolonged, exaggerated or recurrent. Such emotional disturbance impedes learning and the process of teaching. The disruption causes tension which is uncomfortable to the child and those around him. Momentary or brief disturbances occur in all persons with stress. Usually equilibrium is rapidly restored by use of inner controls, after the stress situation is evaluated and ways to cope with the stress have been implemented. With some children who become upset, the disequilibrium remains long after the stress is removed. Their inner controls are rudimentary and their capacity for critical evaluation may be absent due to their disturbance.

The immediate task for the teacher or for the parent then is to assist the disturbed youngster by outer control to reach inner calm and stability. Usually there is some carry-over learning of such internal controls so that a similar stress may be handled better on another occasion. The ultimate goal, of course, is to understand the antecedents causing the disruptive behavior. Frequently and frustratingly such knowledge may not be available and the behavior needs to be modified *without* the full satisfaction of problem analysis. It is important to recognize that many times problem solving is possible and successful without actually ascertaining the underlying causes of the disruptive behavior. This observation is an important finding from use of behavior modification programs.

Unruly behavior, verbal or physical, is a common difficulty to be dealt with in the home, classroom, lunchroom or playground. Immediate coping is important to prevent disturbances of the entire class or a minor epidemic of emotionally distraught children who become anxious or angry and join in.

When the adult is in control, a child rapidly settles down. However when the adult loses emotional control by counter-anger or tears, a child becomes even more upset. It is important to evaluate whether the unruly behavior is provocative—(in search of negative attention) or defensive —(in response to anxiety or some internal emotional problem which the child is as yet unable to express or handle in any other way). At such a time, calm, quiet external control by a verbal command such as "take it easy", "pull yourself together", can rapidly restore self-control to the child. Physical restraint such as a hand on the shoulder or a grip on the wrist also assists the child to regain calm.

Physical violence should be carefully avoided, since then the child's self-preservation reflexes come into play with reciprocal damage. This then is "war", which needs two sides. The controlled adult is in a better position to desist from a declaration of battle. The cooler the emotions of the adult, the more he can assist the fiery excitement of the disturbed child.

When a *small* child totally loses control, the "hold technique" is of great usefulness: the child is contained in the adult lap with the back of the child against the adult's chest; the child's arms crossed left to right over his own chest. The adult grips the child's wrists; the adult's legs should be hooked around the child's ankles; the adult's chin tucked against the child's neck to prevent head-thrashing (and biting). This gives total body contact and containment and can be soothing to the child. Adult tones should be kept low, slow and soft. Almost whisper: "Calm down, stop screaming, calm down." "We can let go when you're calm." Gradually the adults' grip is loosened as the child's control returns. The whole technique may need to be repeated quite a few times in the struggle for control, but should be used only if consistent follow-through is possible. It is most effective and conveys that until the child establishes internal controls for himself, the responsible adult will provide external controls. The lesson is quite dramatically learned this way. It is superior to a general screaming match that often ends with everyone in tears, blame, rejection and helplessness.

Responsible use of punishment, as well as of rewards, is an important task as well as a test of the self-discipline, maturity and leadership of the adult, be he parent, President, policeman, or principal. Responsible adults in leadership positions are constantly in the strong spotlight of the eyes of the young. When the message give is: "Do as I say but not as I do" the result is chaos for discipline in the home or classroom. *Example*: A teenager made a suicide attempt for which psychiatric consultation was called. The girl matter-of-factly stated of her father: "I know he's having an affair, so what right does he have to threaten to throw me out of the house if I get pregnant?" Her period was 2 weeks overdue when she attempted suicide.

Discipline has no easy recipe. It is a slow, lifelong process of taking apart human behavior and evaluating which parts are acceptable and unacceptable, which aspects should be encouraged and which discouraged. Methods to do this have to be tested and tried in the context of each individual, with recognition of strengths and weaknesses, abilities and limitations. There should be sufficient flexibility in every system of rules and laws to allow for differences and exceptional circumstances.

Many are seriously reviewing and revising ancient

71

and traditional rules and laws to fit the needs and creeds of the seventies. Underlying apparent permissiveness is serious testing and evaluation of the multiple dimensions of human behavior. With depth understanding of the way behavior is learned have come ways to undo mistakes and relearn more adaptive behavior. This new psychology takes into account the strengths of physiological human drives, attempting to harness these in the service of the individual.

Discipline, in the sense of following a leader, or of a method of study containing rules and order, is a means by which the learning process is facilitated. A body of knowledge is shared to train novices and develop improved skills.

The more highly developed a discipline has become, the greater its potential for growth and development. With sophistication and growth in the specialty of science and physics, and in collaboration with numerous other disciplines, man has been able to conquer previous limitations of technology and space and finally reach the moon. The entire space program has been highly exacting—of self-discipline as well as of a general collaborative discipline. A sustained standard of excellence had to be maintained by every member of the enormous team. It was a pleasure to watch the teamwork, the steady control of every detail; the mature concern, consideration and responsibility of each individual from astronauts to technicians and TV news commentators. That fantastic endeavor of man reaching the moon should give satisfaction and hope to all. It is a dramatic example of the great height of success attained in the 1970s, in the art of human discipline.

For troubled children, self-discipline is slower in coming. Time, repetition, persistence, understanding, endurance, concern, great amounts of patience, some love, and external structure are the essential ingredients to be used by parents, teachers, and professionals who would assist the child to build a pathway towards comfortable internal control and self-reliance. Special children too, with discipline can achieve the "flame of freedom in their souls, and light of knowledge in their eyes."

Now for a frolic! Now for a leap! Now for a madcap galloping chase! I'll make a commotion in every place!

William Howlitt

6

The Hyperkinetic Child —
Definition and Diagnosis

Anecdotes from early literature from various parts of the world strongly indicate that the hyperkinetic child has been around for a long time, in every part of the globe, in every race, with very similar prevalence. Fairy tales and children's stories through the ages document characters today identifiable as children with hyperkinetic reactions. They are depicted (then as now) as always in trouble, always active, never learning from the disasters precipitated, never little heroes. Their behavior variant of speed and action was recognized as disruptive. A negative value was accorded it in rhymes and tales of "Fidgety Phil", "Harry Hurricane", and "Tommy Tornado".

Speed and action are greatly prized by 20th century man. Supersonic jets and Olympic medals confirm this. The more rapidly their child walks and talks, the prouder the parents. Speed is part of the value system for most urban as well as primitive societies.

The Hyperactive Child

As was mentioned in the introduction, world-wide medical recognition of the entity of the "hyperactive child" belongs to the 20th century. There is a strong drive toward universal literacy for all who live in complex urban societies where reading is essential for daily functioning. Laws now prohibit child labor; agriculture is highly mechanized; the large extended family is more the rarity than the rule. These were all previously resources to absorb and maintain the unschooled. A rural culture had an easy tolerance of illiteracy and numerous viable alternatives. Today good parents are expected to produce educated children, since even the most menial jobs require a capacity to read instructions and write reports of some kind. The hyperkinetic child, with his inability to adjust to the school environment, must now be helped to stay and receive an education, rather than pushed, as in the past, into another alternative.

In 1954, at the International Institute on Child Psychiatry in Toronto, Canada, Maurice W. Laufer, M.D., who had worked in collaboration with Denhoff and Solomons, read his pioneering paper entitled, "Hyperkinetic Impulse Disorder in Children's Behavior Problems." Since then many studies have been directed towards the clinical, academic, and chemical aspects of such children. These studies became possible with the development of additional specialties in medicine such as pediatrics and psychiatry, which focused increasing attention on hyperactive children. They seemed to encompass a wide variety and ranged from mild to severe.

Numerous synonyms used in the United States and

abroad cluttered the literature. No universal nomenclature existed which could assist investigators at an international level. "Choreatiform syndrome", "hyperkinesis in rural Vermont", "choreiform syndrome", "minimal brain dysfunction", "minimal cerebral dysfunction", "hyperkinetic impulse disorder", "hyperkinetic behavior syndrome", "brain-damaged child", and "hyperactive child" catalog a few of 38 or more different titles applied to the phenomena under discussion.

Definition

In an attempt to bring order out of chaos, *The Diagnostic and Statistical Manual of Mental Disorders* of the American Psychiatric Association, in the second edition (DSM-II) in 1968, gave this definition under 308.0: "Hyperkinetic Reaction of Childhood (or Adolescence)":

> This disorder is characterized by hyperactivity, restlessness, distractibility, and short attention span, especially in young children; the behavior usually diminishes in adolescence. If this behavior is caused by organic brain damage, it should be diagnosed under the appropriate non–psychotic Organic Brain Syndrome.

Clarification of the confusion was not greatly assisted. This definition did not clearly differentiate from those children with other behavior disorders who may also show the symptoms of hyperactivity.

The term *"hyperkinetic reaction"* (HK), is used to describe the behavioral component of the syndrome,

79

namely the hyperactivity, distractibility, short attention span. "Minimal brain dysfunction (MBD)" differs in that MBD attempts to describe the *functioning* deficiency between thought processes and learning and motor execution. Minimal brain *damage* implies a clear knowledge that there is indeed damaged brain tissue, which at this point is merely speculative, or sometimes hypothesized from clinical findings where neurological signs are detected. The implications may be that dysfunction can occur without actual tissue damage, or that if there is tissue damage, it is not massive, since there are no "hard" neurological signs present in most cases. No such substantiating evidence is currently available. Therefore the behavioral title: Hyperkinetic Reaction is preferable until further data warrants change.

Diagnosis

The syndrome of "hyperkinetic reaction of childhood" (or adolescence) is a recognizable entity. When its signs are very gross, the problem is easily defined by age 2 years (with development of not only walking, but also of running skills). Usually by the time the child is 2½ years old, the mother is worn out and the family less than tolerant of the child's behavior. By age 3 years, there is doubt that this particular child shows promise of "growing out of it", as the grandparents and family pediatrician, among others, may have said.

The youngest patient brought to the author was a 1½ year old boy, youngest in a sibship of six. The father was a civil engineer, the mother cheerful and sensible. She reported a normal labor but a very rapid delivery. The child developed slowly till age 15 months when he began to run, not having crawled. He had then begun to speak in sentences, not having babbled at all. From then on, "it was like having a hurricane in the house, everything up for grabs". He would climb out of his crib (by 15 months) early in the morning and not fall asleep till midnight. Daytime naps had ceased by 15 months. His activity was ceaseless. He was extremely distractable, never watched TV, never finished a meal without needing to be brought back to his highchair at the table a dozen times. He had no concept of danger, had two greenstick arm fractures from two falls from the same tree (three similar falls resulted in abrasions only). He was considered a "bully" by his sibs and older peers. He did not respond to rewards or punishment. Two pediatricians had declared him "just a boy", and above the 100th percentile for height and weight. This did not help the home situation. A third pediatrician responded to the family's sleep disruption by giving the patient phenobarbital, which made him even *more* hyperactive at night. Finally the parents referred themselves with the patient for psychiatric evaluation. He was indeed "super-hyperkinetic". He responded dramatically to Dextroamiphetamine 2.5 mg. on wakening and at noon. By the third day of treatment he was asleep at 8 P.M. and eating with the family was possible with only two trips away from the table. He is now 6 years old, doing exceptionally well in regular first grade, and is being seen at the clinic at three month intervals.

81

The Hyperactive Child

Usually by about 5 years, expectable age-related "normal" hyperactivity should begin to noticeably decrease. Attention and concentration improve to where the child participates in games with peers; watches TV programs that interest him; finishes a meal (with one or two interruptions), and entertains himself up to 30 to 60 minutes at a time. How then to differentiate?

Symptoms

Recognition of hyperkinetic reaction is not difficult when, by the age of 5 years, at least half of the following signs are persistently and recurrently (not occasionally) present:

1. Ceaseless, purposeless activity
2. Short attention span
3. Highly distractible
4. Highly excitable; labile emotions (from tears to laughter in minutes)
5. Uncontrolled impulses (talks, hits, leaps, etc.)
6. Poor concentration (overincludes *all* stimuli, unable to screen out or discriminate)
7. Heedless of danger/pain
8. Poor response to reward/punishment
9. Destructive; aggressive; lies; steals; has temper tantrums
10. Constant clash with environment (including pets)
11. Accident-prone; clumsy; poor motor-co-ordination
12. Speech problems

13. Strabismus (squint)
14. Perception difficulties; audio-visual problems
15. Mixed L-R dominance (ex: R-handed/L-eyed/R-legged)
16. Irregular developmental milestones (*example*: no crawling then sudden walking; no babbling then sudden sentences)
17. "Untidy" drawing, coloring, handwriting, (overshooting of lines; unable to draw parallel lines; unable to stay within boundaries)
18. Nothing completed spontaneously, needs excess reminders (eat/dress/task)
19. Inability to cope with phase-related activity (*example*: collaborative games, riding bicycle, gym, etc.)
20. Poor socialization; quarrelsome; no respect for needs or property of others; friendless; disruptive.
21. Sleep disturbance
22. Needs constant supervision

The *cluster* of many signs in the child is essential for the diagnosis.

From this listing, many variants of the hyperkinetic reaction of childhood are to be expected and indeed are clinically seen. Not all are as severe as the 1½-year-old patient described. Some hyperkinetic children are well-coordinated. For them sports provide an excellent outlet for their excess activity. Many have no sleep disturbances. Some children with hyperkinetic reaction are exceptionally bright, but are underachievers due to their inability to sustain attention long enough even to be tested or taught. With the help of appropriate medication, they may be assisted to settle down, to learn, and do very well academically.

There is no such specific entity as "*the* hyperkinetic child". Rather it is a wide umbrella diagnosis covering a range from mild to severe. Some children with a hyperkinetic reaction enter a strange room like a tornado, touching and tumbling everything within reach, with little recognition that this behavior is unacceptable. They are unable to contain their tendencies to be stimulated by every sight and sound in their stimulus field. Others may explore only with their eyes, remaining confined in one spot and clingingly afraid near their mother. They constantly move their bodies, however, particularly the large muscle groups. They wriggle and bob up and down, unable to sustain a focus of interest, having to be brought back many times by direction to the immediate task or subject.

If professionals could clearly describe both the behavioral and the functional aspects of the hyperkinetic patient, it would enrich the dimensions of understanding him, as well as contributing to cross-discipline comprehension and collaboration. If a child with hyperkinetic reaction shows, in addition to the hyperkinesis, a specific learning disability such as dyscalculia or visual–perceptual difficulty, or poor audio–visual-motor co-ordination, of sufficient severity to impede functioning, such diagnosis should be carefully added. This would assist correlation of studies from various research centers.

Of particular diagnostic importance is the child's responsiveness to the use of drugs, as well as to specific teaching techniques. Diagnostic trial of medication becomes the burden of responsibility of physician and parent alike, regardless of their prejudices against use of long-term medication for a child. The condition of hyperkinetic reaction is as treatable as juvenile diabetes. A child's right to treatment as early and as adequately as possible, should be respected.

A meaningful diagnostic trial of medication takes time; patience; close contact between parent and physician, teacher and parent, and teacher and physician; objective observation of *changes* in the listing of problems present in the child.

Table I is suggested as helpful for such a diagnostic evaluation. It should be carefully completed by physician, teacher and parent and compared for each specific drug used, if more than one kind of medication needs to be given trial. A rational approach toward chemotherapy is "minimum dose for maximum effect." The *minimum* for a specific child means "optimum to achieve relief." The *same* medication should be slowly increased at three day intervals (provided there are no undesirable effects) over at least a three-week period before a decision is made to stop that and to try another. The questionnaire should be *repeated for each increase*. The same protocol and cooperation is again required in evaluating the new medication, using the same careful feedback regarding changes.

This procedure is time consuming for the first few weeks, but has high long-range dividends for physician, parent and teacher. Since the therapeutic approach is much different for conditions confused with hyperkinetic reaction, diagnostic clarity is essential in management.

Differential Diagnosis

To be excluded from this diagnostic category of hyperkinetic reaction are other conditions, some already described at length, which show hyperactivity as one of many symptoms in their symptom cluster.

The Psychotic Child

Such a child shows severe and intense inner turmoil with disintegration of functioning. The internal anxiety may cause *under*-responsiveness to stimuli, rather than the excessive responsiveness in HK. There may be *un*-understandable bizarre behavior; stereotyped movements with marked sameness from which the psychotic child is *not distractible*. There is usually an unsatisfactory response to a diagnostic trial of stimulants. In some rare instances a psychotic child may show true hyperkinesis additionally. Such cases respond better to major tranquillizers which have anti-psychotic properties as well as sedative effects.

The Overanxious Reaction of Childhood

The overanxious child displays pseudo-hyperkinetic behavior which is really an anxiety-equivalent. There are small plucking movements of hands and feet rather than whole leg and buttock body movements. The child's own attention is usually sustained, but pent-up tension is evident. Such hyperactivity is easily reversible upon reassurance or capture of interest by the examiner or authority person. The child can then control the hyperactive movements. Trial of stimulants is of no or aggravating effect.

Unsocialized Aggressive Reaction

This is perhaps the most consistently confused with hyperkinetic reaction. On close scrutiny, it will be seen that the hyperactivity, aggression, violence, and destructiveness of the unsocialized child are definitely purposive. The child concentrates before, during, and after the act of aggression. Between aggressive outbursts, there is sustained attention, the child is not distractible, and there is usually an absence of neurological components.

Normal Constitutional Hyperactivity

The normal hyperactivity of children from two to five is described in Chapter II.

Seizure Variants

Unrecognized seizure variants may take the form of recurrent "tics" of the face; tonic-clonic foot and hand movements; "absences" of attention. These combine to give "inattention" and involuntary muscle jerks. The dramatic grand mal seizure with loss of consciousness, involuntary urination, and subsequent sleep is easily identified; it is the subtle variants of epilepsy that need to be excluded by EEG. These seizure variants usually respond well to anti-convulsant medication, but not to trial of stimulants.

87

The Hyperactive Child

Sydenham's Chorea

This syndrome, described in 1685, follows acute rheumatic fever. It has a sudden onset in children between five and fifteen, and affects girls more often than boys. The child, who was not previously hyperactive, begins to show recurrent flailing movements of arms and legs, facial contortions, and swallowing difficulty. The symptoms are dramatic and usually disappear in about 3 months without specific treatment.

Post-traumatic Organic Brain Syndrome

After recovery from a head injury, a child may be observed to show the clinical picture of hyperkinetic reaction. Very careful documentation of previous functioning, including teacher's reports, should be obtained. It must be remembered that children with hyperkinetic reaction are accident-prone, heedless of danger, and often fall from heights and run across highways. The hyperkinetic condition might be the cause rather than the result of the head injury. Litigation may be involved, making previous history important in establishing cause and effect.

Encephalitic Organic Brain Syndrome

This syndrome is reported as occurring preliminary to a clinical picture of hyperkinetic reaction. Medical records and previous history assist in establishing the diagnosis and etiology. After the 1918 United States epidemic of encephalitis, Holman in 1922, at Johns Hopkins, wrote case reports on post-encephalitic behavior disorders in children. In the 1930's, Bond followed up with a series of papers on post-encephalitic children, while Bradley used stimulant drugs on the same children to assist their clinical deficity.

This author has been consulted in three similar cases, all males 5 to 6 years old, all at 6 months after the acute episode. There were other neurological residues. None of the children responded well to a trial of stimulants. All three showed improvement on major tranquillizers, together with anti-convulsants to control their post-encephalitic seizures. This is a complex area meriting further research, since little is documented in recent medical literature.

Mental Retardation

The mentally retarded child, with or without psychosis, may show constant activity. On study the behavior is perseverative in nature, unchanging for hours. Attention is short, but the child is *not* distractible. Often he does *not* respond to stimuli, concentrating on the same repetitive activity he has chosen. Retardation is evident in development, intelligence, speech, and self-care.

Toxic Organic Brain Syndrome

This syndrome is acute and may be due to drugs or alcohol abuse. Chronic toxic brain syndrome is seen in chronic lead poisoning. Stored lead can give blood levels above 24.5 mg/100 cc., as found by David in a study of

89

TABLE I*
RATING SCALE
Clinic/Physician Title

Child: _____ Age: _____ Date: _____

Medication: _____

Problem-list. Please rate your observation as follows:
Impossible—3; much worse—2; Same 0; Better + 1; Much better + 2;
Absent + 3.

	Mother	Teacher	Physician
1. Hyperactive body movements			
2. Attention Span (eating, TV)			
3. Distractability			
4. Concentration			
5. Impulsiveness			
6. Destructiveness			
7. Aggressiveness			
8. Lying			
9. Stealing			
10. Awareness of danger			

11. Response to punishment
12. Emotional stability
13. Clumsiness
14. Accident-proneness
15. Motor co-ordination (games, gym)
16. Speech Problem
17. Perception-understanding
18. Making friends
19. Quarrelsomeness
20. Drawing
21. Handwriting
22. Reading
23. Calculations
24. Problem-solving capacity
25. Temper Tantrums
26. Self-Reliance
27. Completes projects
28. Eating Problems
29. Mealtime disruption
30. Sleep Problems

The Hyperactive Child

over 100 eight-year-olds, a few with an early history of inadequately treated lead ingestion. The chelating agent penecillamine is the treatment of choice.

Chronic barbituate use, by legitimate medical prescription, may worsen the condition of such organic hyperactivity.

Reversibility and improvement may be expected if ingestion has not been in near-lethal doses. Six weeks to six months should be allowed for optimum detoxification. Active anti-toxin may not be used for all of that time, but the body's restorative capacity, which is usually good in a healthy child, cannot be adequately evaluated by immediate observation alone. Longitudinal observation over at least six months is necessary.

Oh! Why am I what I am
And why am I anything?
Am I not as wild as the wind
Why? Why?

Anonymous

7

The Hyperkinetic Child — Epidemiology, Pathology and Work-up

In the effort to master his environment, man has from the earliest recorded times scrutinized and mapped the problems and positive points of his own and other known territories. From such curiosity, the science of epidemiology emerged. Gathering details of incidence, vulnerable age groups, sex differences, families with above average incidence, overall prevalence, and cyclical epidemics of a disease all give greater depth to understanding of the phenomenon being studied. Further dimension is afforded by careful study of underlying pathology, so that causal factors may be accurately determined; then hopefully a "cure" may be discovered. Ideally, when all of these steps have been successfully followed, research should come through with the final anti-illness weapon—prevention—like the dramatic smallpox vaccine.

Such dramatic answers to medical mysteries, however, are historically infrequent. More commonly we find the "cure" or good treatments long before all of the other parts of the puzzle are known. Much more is known about how to treat hyperkinetic reaction than about *why* it occurs. Nonetheless, an orderly outline of what knowledge is currently available assists new workers in the field to continue to work on the problems.

Epidemiology

Prevalence

Accuracy of the statistics of the estimations regarding prevalence (existing cases) of hyperkinetic reaction is affected by inevitable difficulty due to the described diagnostic confusion. One statistic states "three million MBD in the U.S." In 1966, a group reported 4% prevalence in St. Louis grade school children between the ages of five and eleven. In Vermont in 1967, a prevalence of 10% was reported, and in 1970 in Maryland, 20% of elementary school children were reported to have problems of restlessness and short attention span.

Incidence

Most workers in the field would accept a figure of a current incidence rate (new cases) of 6% to 10% of hyperkinetic reaction in children below the age of 10.

Defined Populations

World-wide prevalence of hyperkinetic reaction is reported. Studies are in progress in both rural and urban communities.

Genetic Factors

No studies of monozygotic twin concordance for hyperkinetic reaction are known to this author. Clinicians anecdotally report an occasional family where each of two brothers shows hyperkinetic reaction and responds similarly to stimulants. Wender reports an unpublished study by D. J. Safer on the familiar incidence of MBD, revealing that 50% of sibs of the MBD child show short attention span and hyperactivity. This author has three families in active treatment with two boys per family objectively diagnosed to be hyperkinetic and individually responding well to stimulant medication.

Epidemics

The factor of post infectious encephalitic hyperkinesis stimulated the earliest scientific consideration as a clinical entity. The work of the 1920s and 1930s by Hohman and Bond should be re-evaluated and followed up. Could there be an immunological factor operant?

Sex Ratio

The male:female 4:1 sex ratio shows a clear sex linkage for hyperkinetic reaction of childhood. This roughly parallels the observed sex ratio for other childhood psychiatric disorders.

Pathology

As yet, no specific histological entity has been shown or accepted to be "the specific" etiological pathology of hyperkinetic reaction of childhood. The entities discussed below are all still in the hypothetical or speculative phase of thinking.

Minimal Brain Damage

This concept takes into account:
1. Prenatal intrauterine factors such as maternal illnesses—rubella; toxoplasmosis; virus; anemia; malnutrition; diabetes mellitis; pre-eclamptic toxemia; hypertension; thyrotoxicosis; circulatory insufficiency; respiratory problems—which could affect the fetus.
2. Concern has been expressed regarding delivery of infants by terminating pregnancy, inducing labor, initiating uterine contractions, and, for convenience, artificially controlling the entire delivery procedure. No documentation of specific cerebral damage is recorded. Long-range effects on the infant of the specific medications used for control of labor are under scrutiny and study for possible causal connection between induction of labor and later problems in the child.
3. Birth trauma, either mechanical or anoxic, is inescapable in the separation process of childbirth, by whatever route. Emergence is a high risk venture for the fetus. In severe cases that succumb to delivery difficulties, scattered cerebral gray matter, petechial hemorrhages, and

98

microscopic focal loss of tissue in the brain are found at post mortem.

At Harvard, 600 such neonatal cases were studied by Towbin, who reported five main forms of central nervous system damage: subdural hemorrhage; spinal cord and brainstem damage; hypoxic damage to deep cerebral structures (particularly in prematures); hypoxic damage to the cerebral cortex; and hypoxic damage to *deep* structures of brainstem in premature neonates. It is hypothesized that in hyperkinetic reaction, the brain has minimal variants of cerebral pathology. No hard evidence is currently available.

Minimal Brain Dysfunction

As in minimal brain damage, above, this concept is based on a presumption of anatomic causes underlying behavioral difficulties.

"Immaturity" of Brain Tissue

This theory postulates that hyperkinetic reaction is due to prematurity or low birth weight. The premise is that the pathology therefore is based on inadequate myelinization of the central nervous system. This myelinization allegedly does occur, although belatedly, in hyperkinetic reaction, and so accounts for the "growing out" phenomenon seen at puberty or a little before puberty. There is no hard evidence to substantiate this theory at this time. Clinically, however, a large percentage of those with hyperkinetic reaction show growth, maturation and improved general control.

Post-natal Stress

Trauma to the head; encephalitis; endocrine or metabolic diseases are postulated to cause "mild brain damage." Upon recovery, hyperkinetic behavior reactions are noted in children previously *not* noted to have had such behavior. The exact pathology is as yet not documented, but is postulated to be on the basis of scattered microscopic lesions. Specific anatomical sites are being sought.

From animal experiments two areas are incriminated:

1. The median forebrain bundle which runs most of the length of the brain in mammals (Olds, 1962). This site responds optimally to electrical stimulation and is related to reinforcement and avoidance, which are both important in learning through rewards and punishments. This learning capacity is seemingly absent in children with hyperkinetic reactions.

2. The caudate nucleus, which is closely related to the endocrine system (Olds, 1958). This may account for the puberty improvement in children with hyperkinetic reactions. The work has not yet been substantiated in humans, nor is it as yet widely accepted.

Research continues for "*the* anatomic site" of the postulated "brain damage" in hyperkinetic reaction.

Biochemical Basis for Pathology

A more acceptable direction for current research is the investigation of a biological basis for hyperkinetic reaction.

Great perplexity is generated by the "paradoxical response" of children with hyperkinetic reaction to amphetamines. Children with hyperkinetic reaction metabolize amphetamines in a different way than normal children. The end result of such metabolism is that the stimulant activity of the amphetamine is *not* observed. It acts instead paradoxically in a tranquillizing manner; dramatically calming the overactive behavior of the child; increasing concentration and learning; reducing distractibility.

It is postulated that the amphetamines act on the reticular area of the brain stem (which controls consciousness and attention) by stimulating both the reticular activating system and the reticular inhibitory system. Action of the reticular inhibitory system serves to balance the activating system, so that the brain of the child is not flooded by reactions to every verbal, visual, or auditory stimulus. Concentration and learning then become possible due to the screening out or filtering by the inhibitory system.

Such regulation of this reticular area of the brainstem is believed to be due changes in the catecholamine—acetylcholine index in brain tissue. In rats, if the catecholamine nor-epinephrine is injected into the reticular

101

system, it lowers general activity. In humans, norepinephrine controls transmission at nerve endings. Dextroamphetamine affects the metabolism of norepinephrine. It is speculated that very high or very low levels of catecholamines produce hyper-arousal, (therefore hyperkinesis) but intermediate amounts allow for normal activity and arousal.

Another incidental finding in a small series is of interest. Hyperkinetic children of parents with manic-depressive illness respond by slowing down to lithium carbonate, similar to the way that the parents respond to lithium carbonate in the hypo-manic phase of their illness. A strong genetic factor on a biochemical basis is believed to be operant here.

Researchers seem to be on the verge of a breakthrough regarding the chemical mysteries of the hyperkinetic reactions. It will, however, take many years of careful, close, longitudinal follow-up of these children before we begin to understand whether we are dealing with a homogeneous population or many very different biochemical phenomena.

Diagnostic Work-up

Ideally, the full evaluation of a child should include:

Parent Evaluation

    1. Family History
    2. Child's Medical History:
       immunizations, hospitalizations, childhood diseases, injuries.

3. Child's Developmental History:
   Pregnancy (any maternal problems), delivery, neonatal problems, milestones (smiled, flipped, sat, used words, crawled, used sentences, walked, ran, climbed stairs, knew colors, fed self, dressed self, tied shoelaces, toilet-trained, caught ball).
4. Child's Behavioral History:
   Covering the 21 problems listed earlier under Diagnosis.

Teacher Evaluation

1. Report of Learning Capacity:
   Speech, reading, arithmetic, writing, gym.
2. Report of Behavior:
   Again covering the 21 problems listed under Diagnosis.
3. Report of School Psychologicals:
   Perceptual or audio-visual difficulties.

Physician Evaluation

1. Pregnancy History:
   Maternal illness, medications, bleeding, malnutrition, anemia, diabetes, hypertension, toxemia, thyroid problems, fetal movements (if excessive, as reported by some mothers for their child with hyperkinetic reaction), full term or premature, other pregnancies.
2. Birth History:
   Duration of labor, anesthetic used, caesarean section, use of forceps, episiotomy, excess bleeding, oxygen, blood transfusion, pitocin induction of

labor, fetal distress, cord around neck, position (breech or posterior), infant's condition (Apgar at 1-5 minutes).

3. Neonatal History:
   Incubator, sucking, crying, general condition, weight on discharge.

4. Developmental History:
   Sensorimotor, social interactional, language, adaptive capacity, cognitive development, physical (height, weight), pathology (illnesses, injuries).

5. Behavioral History:
   Covering the 21 problems listed earlier under Diagnosis.

6. Family History:
   Marital status, siblings, psychiatric problems (alcoholism, sociopathy, hysteria), learning difficulties in other family members.

7. Full Physical Examination:
   Including careful *neurological* examination, to include scrutiny of such so-called "soft" neurological signs indicative of hyperkinetic reaction as *clusters* of the following signs:

   –occasional speech disorders

   –poorly controlled volume of speech

   –unstable body balance with eyes shut

   –difficulty in walking toe-heel along a straight line

   –accessory movements while walking toe-heel along a straight line

104

—"drift" of outstretched arm-hands with eyes closed
—dysmetria or difficulty with finger-nose test
—dysdiadokinesis or clumsy rapid hand movements
—difficulty with fine motor coordination—doing buttons, shoelaces, dressing and undressing
—gait incoordination
—nystagmus or involuntary movements of the eyes
—difficulty with oculomotor "following"
—inability to do rapid sequential touch of all four fingers of same hand to thumb
—tremors
—choreiform accessory movements
—overextension of arms at the elbow when walking tip-toe
—synkinesis or mirror movements of opposite side of body when one side is tested
—mixed right-left dominance of eyes/hands/legs
—directional confusion
—stereognosis or inability to recognize objects placed in palm with eyes closed
—graphaesthesia or inability to recognize letters or numbers written on palm or skin with eyes closed
—simultagnosia or inability to define two touch stimuli given simultaneously at different parts of body
—hyperreflexia

–occasional unilateral Babinski (upgoing toe reflex)

–slight unsustained clonus

–drawing difficulties: inability to stay within or to copy parallel lines; distorts or rotates copied geometrical shapes as on Bender-Gestalt test

–constructional apraxia or inability to copy block designs

No single sign is pathognomonic, but the presence of at least four or five is significant.

8. Lab Tests:

Routine blood and urine exams, skull x-ray if trauma or intracranial masses are suspected, EEG.

Electroencephalography is expensive, needs serial follow-ups, and may be of value, particularly in ruling out seizure disorders which require specific treatment. It may show up focal discharges diagnostic of subdurals or of masses. It may be "non-specific abnormal" as it is in 10-30% of "normal" elementary school children and 30-80% of hyperkinetic reaction children. The very wide range in reported percentages reflects a still controversial state concerning its specificity in hyperkinetic reaction.

Total reliance on EEG for diagnosis is a medical mistake. For completeness of a thorough medical work-up, an EEG should be done. However, if financial reasons preclude use of the test, treatment should not be delayed. Stimulant therapy will not alter the EEG if done later.

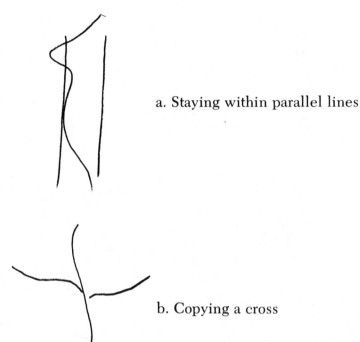

a. Staying within parallel lines

b. Copying a cross

c. Primitive body-image in drawing of self

Figure I. Drawings by a 7½ year old boy with hyperkinetic reaction (pre-treatment)

9. Speech Evaluation:
   Should be done if indicated, to identify what type of speech therapy could assist. The earlier speech therapy is started, the less likelihood of formation of fixed patterns of poor articulation with all its resultant effects of teasing, name calling, personal frustrations, and rejections.
10. Psychological Testing:
    Should be done by psychologist skilled in working with children. Evidence of fine organicity may show up on a WISC, Rorschach, Bender-Gestalt, figure drawings, or black design tests. Visual motor, audio-visual perceptual disorders should be carefully documented, with specific remedial recommendations for teachers. School psychologists usually provide such expertise. Where this service is not available through the schools, good psychometrics, although expensive, should be obtained, since they are of inestimable value in assisting with a clearer understanding of the child's learning difficulties.
11. Diagnostic Trial of Medication:
    Covered earlier under Diagnosis.

*It is well to give when asked
but it is better to give unasked
through understanding*

Kahlil Gibran

8

The Hyperkinetic Child — Management and Treatment

From an understanding of the many behavioral difficulties of children with hyperkinetic reactions, a rational approach to their management must include child, family, school, and medication. This necessitates a complex interdisciplinary network for each child.

For emphasis, it is repeated that management will take time; persistence; endurance; understanding; concern; patience and much structure. Patience, love, special teaching facilities and specific medications are all added bonuses.

The Child

The examining physician should ask the child why he thinks he has been brought for examination, for the purposes of establishing how the child sees himself and his problem. He should always be told, *at his maturational level* of cognitive functioning, what the examining physician thinks. *Example*: "It seems you have to keep moving and moving because you have a very active nervous system. . . ." Also tell him what plans are being made. "I have asked your parents to give you one thing at a time to do," "we will try to get you into a special classroom with only 8 children instead of 30, so you can get extra help," or "we will have your mother give you some medication to help you slow down a bit . . . ," "you will really have to work with all of us to see you do not get into trouble as much. . . ."

This approach is suitable for children from 3 to 13 years. One common error adults make is to talk *about* the child in his presence rather than *to* him. Good direct eye-to-eye contact allows the child to begin to know, trust, even like the adult, which enhances his responses and cooperation.

At this age, independence is rudimentary. Little can be done without the family and school upon whom he is still at least 85% dependent for survival. If he is thrown out of school after school, he becomes a "second grade dropout" as one 8-year-old presented himself. Before or without special education facilities, these children did indeed drop out of the main stream of life.

Rejected by the school system, the next rejection was from the home to the children's wards of state hospitals. Institutionalizing prevailed as recently as 1960, and some children have remained in institutions for years, merely contained—untreated, uneducated, unloved. In the 1970s, this mismanagement is inexcusable. There are resources which can and should be extended to assist children with Hyperkinetic Reactions to their optimum human potential.

In management of the child, recognize whether he has any combination of these problems:

Personal Problems

Inability to sustain control of his ceaseless activity; irregular physical growth; difficulty controlling sphincters, bowel or bladder; difficulties with body image, right-left confusion; visual problems; squint; "pseudo-deafness" due to inattention; coordination difficulties; greater need for masturbation.

Social Problems

Problems controlling *all* of his emotions and behavior in public; disruptiveness; inability to collaborate; failure to complete tasks; no friends; provoking anger and rejection; aggression; failure to engage in "constructive" play (which is where most of the "work" of learning occurs in childhood); tendency to become the family scapegoat.

Emotional Problems

Lability (from tears to laughter in minutes); overreaction to humor; frustration on correction; use of acting-out of anger or pain (usually in shouting or tantrum behavior) as main coping device; episodes of sadness and depression which may be fleeting but recurrent.

113

The Hyperactive Child

Academic Problems

IQ lower than true capacity due to distractibility and inattention at time of testing; mixed dominance (right-left cross-over eye/hand/leg); reading, writing, arithmetic difficulties; problems with cognition; problems with audio-visual or visual-motor perception, or both; language problems; poor control of volume and cadence of speech; articulation problems; overinclusion of all classroom stimuli; inability to screen or filter out important from unimportant; avoidance of gym due to coordination and collaboration problems; disruptive behavior on playground because of inability to play or failure to learn games; masturbation in class; bringing to school all the personal, emotional and social problems.

The Family

For better or for worse, the family must survive in order to maintain its members. Each family has its own potentials and limitations. Sudden crises may unite or disrupt family members. So may ongoing, everyday, seemingly endless stress. Alcoholism, debilitating disease, poverty, gross parental marital conflict, severe personality problems of one member are some such chronic stresses. A child with hyperkinetic reaction may provide such an ongoing stress.

To survive, although in disequilibrium, there may be "splits", as some family members unite against others. For the disruptive child with hyperkinetic reaction, his field of orbit is solitary—unless he makes impact with others by

114

collision. Such collision is frequent. Although the parents may love the child, counter-collision is inevitable, simply because their endurance is humanly limited.

The child stimulates recurrent negative reactions in parents, who then begin to have an additional burden of guilt for their frustrations and frequent rejections. Parents may repeatedly resolve to use patience and start anew, only to have old patterns of mayhem duplicated. There is *no* "uninvolved" family member in the family of a child with Hyperkinetic Reaction. Grandparents and neighbors criticize and condemn the parents for "spoiling the boy"; no longer invite the whole family over; refuse to baby-sit; preach about how "I would beat him if he were mine". These may all be part of the antecedent family drama, before the child reaches the office of professional after professional in search of understanding and substantial help.

A family conference is an essential part of management, preferably in the very first week, to complete the professional evaluation. No child exists in a vacuum, nor is there (in most cases) an exclusive dyad with the mother. Fathers are very important and greatly influential, even when totally absent or away for long hours. The fantasy-father that exists in the mind of every child is greater, stronger, tougher and often very different from father in the flesh. How his mother perceives and presents father or his absence influences the child's image of the father.

The physician should make extra efforts to get the father in and evaluate his thinking about the child; whether he perceives a problem in the child or whether he blames his wife; what his reaction is to a suggestion of long-term

115

use of medications; to changes in interactions with the child; to further specialized testing; to possible classroom changes. The father should be encouraged to express his objections openly, to raise questions and to offer some thoughts of his own on management.

With the whole family present, including the child with hyperkinetic reaction, the physician should again outline the findings and plans as simply as possible, allowing time for every member to speak out.

A supportive posture is important. It is important to let the family know by saying so, that the physician:

1. does not blame but understands that it has been very difficult for every member, including the patient.

2. predicts treatment will be a long, bumpy road that will require effort and co-operation from all.

3. knows medication will help but not completely

4. has studied this condition and knows that the child is *not* deliberately hyperkinetic, but that he has a more active nervous system. (as have 3 million other such children), which will respond to certain medications, which will be tried.

5. expects that like every other family member, the hyperkinetic child will have to take full consequences of all of his behavior and learn to earn his privileges.

6. expects them all to act as helpers by thinking out ways to reduce excess stimulation and provide repeated, *clear* but not harsh, external

116

controls till the hyperkinetic child can learn to control himself from within.

7. knows they have had social difficulties as well as ongoing obligations. They are necessarily better able than the physician to select which events to avoid and how to attempt enjoyable substitutes.

8. suggests exploiting any resources such as talents in members or the patient to assist the weaknesses, *example*: one-to-one tolerant teaching of swimming (excellent fun, exercise for co-ordination) or sports so the hyperkinetic child can practice in private with supervision until he has the skills to participate in a small group.

9. assures them that he will remain their doctor, be available for consultation with the school, and see them at regular intervals.

What of the many families where there may be divorce or individual pathology in parents? And what of child rejecting or medication rejecting families? These are hard, often impossible for even the most dedicated professional to treat. What is needed is "social engineering", which is the product of decades of storm, hopefully entering a period of stability.

Calling upon court authorities to place a child elsewhere may at times satisfy the righteous feelings of the professional. However, the chance for follow-up is usually lost. The problem may merely be shifted from one spot to another.

Placement in foster homes or institutions should only

be a *last resort.* Every effort should first be made to pull together the fragmented network available to the child.

The remnants of the family should be gathered, as already described. Visiting nurses might be asked to give support to a harassed mother at home. A social worker from public aid (if applicable) might be contacted in crises for appropriate intervention work with the mother in the home in order to reinforce any attempts she makes to regain stability. The teacher, who may with the mother's consent follow the physician's orders and dispense two doses of medication every school day, can furnish feedback reports of the child's progress (see Table II).

All of this is hard work, but such interdisciplinary efforts can restore some stability to the family. Much information has been shared, but much will be forgotten by the family. The need for some tangible reinforcement has prompted many workers in the field to devise explanatory pamphlets which may be "taken home" and hopefully read again and again. With each reading, the family may be able to note one more item of value.

Embarking on a "medication only" plan is fraught with disaster. Information to be emphasized for parents, sibs, and babysitters of the hyperkinetic child may take the form of this listing given below:

Family Helps for the Child with Hyperkinetic Reaction

1. Be carefully consistent in rules and discipline.
2. Keep your own voice quiet and slow. Anger is normal. Anger can be controlled. Anger does not mean you do not love a child.

118

3. Try hard to keep your emotions cool by bracing for expectable turmoil. Recognize and respond to any positive behavior, however small. If you search for good things, you will find a few.

4. Avoid a ceaselessly negative approach: "Stop"--- "Don't"---"No"---

5. Separate *behavior* which you may not like, from the child's *person*, which you like, e.g.: "I like you. I don't like your tracking mud through the house."

6. Have a very clear routine for this child. Construct a timetable for waking, eating, play, TV, study, chores and bedtime. Follow it flexibly although he disrupts it. Slowly your structure will reassure him until he develops his own.

7. Demonstrate new or difficult tasks, using action accompanied by short, clear, quiet, explanations. Repeat the demonstration until learned. This uses audio-visual-sensory perceptions to reinforce the learning. The memory traces of a hyperkinetic child take longer to form. Be patient and repeat.

8. Try a separate room or a part of a room which is his own special area. Avoid brilliant colors or complex patterns in decor. Simplicity, solid colors, minimal clutter, and a worktable facing a blank wall away from distractions assist concentration. A hyperkinetic child cannot "filter" out overstimulation himself yet.

9. Do one thing at a time: give him one toy from a

119

closed box; clear the table of everything else when coloring; turn off the radio/TV when he is doing homework. Multiple stimuli prevent his concentration from focusing on his primary task.

10. Give him *responsibility*, which is essential for growth. The task should be within his capacity, although the assignment may need much supervision. *Acceptance* and recognition of his efforts (even when imperfect) should not be forgotten.

11. Read his pre-explosive warning signals. Quietly intervene to avoid explosions by distracting him or discussing the conflict calmly. Removal from the battle zone to the sanctuary of his room for a few minutes is useful.

12. Restrict playmates to one or at most two at one time, because he is so excitable. *Your* home is more suitable, so you can provide structure and supervision. Explain your rules to the playmate and briefly tell the other parent your reasons.

13. Do not pity, tease, be frightened by, or overindulge this child. He has a special condition of the nervous system which is manageable.

14. Know the name and dose of his medications. Give these regularly. Watch and remember the effects to report back to your physician.

15. Openly discuss any fears you have about the use of medications with your physician.

16. Lock up all medications, including these, to avoid accidental misuse.

17. Always supervise the taking of medication, even

if it is routine over a long period of years. Responsibility remains with the parents! One day's supply at a time can be put in a regular place and checked routinely as he becomes older and more self-reliant.

18. Share your successful "helps" with his teacher. The outlined ways to help your hyperkinetic child are as important to him as diet and insulin are to a diabetic child.

The School

Teachers merit a verbal bouquet for the marathon they have done and are doing for children with hyperkinetic reactions. In the past they have had little sympathy and no support from parents or principals who tried to blame and shame teachers for "not being able to handle" their classes. Today estimates state that from 5% to 20% of elementary school children show disorders of attention and excess restlessness. A few hundred thousand teachers therefore must be as familiar as the family with the frustrations and defeat of trying to teach and manage the child with hyperkinetic reaction.

In a regular crowded classroom, how did the teacher handle Jumping Joe and Wiggly Willie, Hurricane Harold and Tornado Tom? With the dunce's cap a century ago; with "corridor duty"; with the principal's office; with suspensions; with despair!

Widespread, general recognition of this syndrome is barely ten years old. It was only unfolding as a recognized entity in medical literature in the mid-1950s. It is therefore a tribute to the resourcefulness of the school system of the United States that resources have so rapidly become available in the way of teachers trained in techniques of teaching children with behavioral difficulties, learning problems, and emotional problems, and special smaller classrooms where such techniques and closer supervision with greater individual attention can be utilized.

Community resistance to placement in special education classrooms is a problem. The "visible differences" of classroom size and special yellow school buses make easy targets for teasing. Child and family smart and suffer. This reality cannot be erased. It takes time and testing for things to settle down, for Joe and Willie, Harold and Tom to trust the teacher, to begin learning, to control impulsive behavior—and improve. The bus and classroom become identified and defended as "mine". Parents are reassured as their child improves and learns. Occasional blow-ups recur, but no more than the quota expectable for the child's age. The family and the child adapt to the teasing, realizing that the problem belongs to those who do the namecalling—who are anxious and ignorant of special needs.

The teacher is regarded by this author as "teacher-healer" because the teacher is often the primary therapist in effecting change and improvement in a child with hyperkinetic reaction. Up to 6 hours daily of intense interaction is an effective therapeutic medium. By understanding and respecting the difficulties and limitations, as well as the strengths and skills, of the child, the teacher is

122

able to guide him towards optimum potential performance related to his particular phase of development.

A careful psychological test analysis is an invaluable aid to the teacher, who needs to define the child's problems broadly in terms of hyperactive behavior, inability to attend and concentrate, and underlying learning difficulties.

School psychologists can gather meaningful data to assist the teacher, provided the hyperactive child can cooperate with the examiner. Testing is usually done along these lines:

Motor Functions

> Neurological report
> Lincoln-Oseretsky test of motor development
> Motor inhibition tests

General Intelligence

> WISC
> Maze test
> Drawings

Achievement

> Gray oral reading test
> Wide-range achievement test

Visual-Auditory Perception

> Frosting developmental test of visual perception
> Bender-Gestalt visual-motor test
> Auditory discrimination and synthesis

The Hyperactive Child

Language Functions

> Speech evaluation
> Illinois test of psycholinguistic abilities

Memory

> Story recall
> Benton visual recall
> Sentence memory recall

Emotions

> Despert fables
> Three wishes
> Rorshach
> TAT for children

School counsellors can assist the teacher by helping build the hyperkinetic child's self-esteem, listening to his complaints and assisting him to articulate rather than act out his anger. The counsellor can give reinforcement, supply simple explanations to questions, and help resolve intrapersonal or intrapsychic problems as these arise. Where there is no school counsellor, a school social worker usually assists. In many school settings such a service is not available, so the teacher has to provide the needed exchange in addition to her academic task.

The hyperkinetic child arrives at school loaded with blame, criticism and rejection. Until he is satisfactorily stabilized on medication and able to cope in a regular classroom, the child with hyperkinetic reaction is a candidate for a small special education classroom. Distractions there can be kept minimal. An opaque screen can be placed around his desk, turning it into an "office" where he can "work in peace". This technique recognizes the child's difficulty, and is not used as a punishment.

Assignments for a hyperkinetic child should be short. One page of work at a time is realistic to his capacity for concentration. If the teacher further structures his activity by having him come up to her desk with the completed page to obtain the next single page she encourages completion of each task, and also allows the child some acceptable motor discharge within the classroom.

Recognition of warning signals preliminary to angry outbursts is important to the teacher in class as well as to the mother at home. Mother and teacher should share whatever observations and interventions assist the child to prevent explosions. If a gym or a playground is available and practical, it may be tried, with caution. Sometimes the large unstructured space may "escalate" the hyperactivity, rather than simply allow an outlet. In such a case, setting limits by using one corner only of the playground provides a workable compromise.

Bus drivers are a "silent minority" who merit special honorable mention. Usually their load consists of a heterogenous group of 10 to 30 children, from diverse classrooms, with a variety of problems. Frequently there are flint-and-tinder dyads who regularly disrupt the entire busload of children, cause near traffic disaster and high levels of anger in the driver. Some drivers stop the bus and yell, or use judo or just silently park till the mayhem abates. One bus driver left bus, keys and children a block

The Hyperactive Child

from the school and has not been seen since! It is an unenviable task that requires, in some instances, presence of a bus driver aide to allow for safe driving.

Suggestions for All Concerned Adults

1. Increase the child's self-esteem by avoiding recurrent failure. Start with tasks well within his maturational learning capacity so he can succeed.
2. Give immediate non-verbal recognition, as well as verbal/written rewards or tokens.
3. Use association cues liberally to sustain interest and improve memory retention.
4. Innovate according to perceived problems and skills of the child.
5. Capture interest and improve motivation by controlled and creative use of novelty and surprise.
6. Set some intermediate goals to teach the "effort-achievement" principle.
7. Avoid "overloading" with data. Short but repeated input is more successful.
8. Use audio-visual aids whenever available. They improve cross-sensory association and comprehension.
9. Ask and ask again from administration for teaching materials and media that would help the child learn.
10. Observe and document in writing the pattern of a new child's behavior for about 2 weeks to obtain some depth understanding of his function.

*TABLE I**
SCHOOL MEDICATION CONSENT
AND DIRECTIONS

Parent Permission: Date _____
Child_____ Birthdate _____
Address_____ Phone_____
School_____Grade ___ Teacher_____
                          _____

I hereby consent for the above-named school to supervise the medication prescribed below by my physician for my child.

                      _____

Physician's Direction: Date _____
Child: _____
Medication & Instruction_____

Doctor Requests teacher's comments:
Please observe the following _____

Phone No: _____Best time to call_____

                    _____
                    Physician's Signature
                    Physician/Clinic Name
                    Address_____

* *May be reproduced without author's consent.*

11. For a hyperkinetic child twelve five-minute assignments achieve more than two half-hour ones.
12. Call for psychological consultation through the principal or special education director when perplexed or at a stalemate. Sometimes the eyes stop seeing when they look too hard! A different perspective helps.
13. Request evaluation of hyperkinetic child for transfer from a regular to a special education classroom when he cannot be contained, even with careful teacher effort, good parent contact and medications. The right to learn of 29 other children is usually also at stake.
14. Stay in close touch with the child's physician by regular reports and occasional phone calls. Ideally also by regular psychiatric consultation to teachers in special education classrooms.
15. Try to set aside regularly some special time, although brief, to re-create self. Start a new day with purpose and optimism.

These are all important aspects of assisting the hyperkinetic child as he grows to maturity. They should not be underestimated as the main method of management when used without medication, nor should they be omitted when medication is used. A tendency to view a pill as a "magic cure" is still part of human thinking. The use of medication should always be placed in proper and rational perspective. A body of knowledge has been accumulating regarding a variety of medications used to improve the core problems of hyperkinetic children, namely their ceaseless motor activity and their inability to concentrate. The literature, although vast, is not always illuminating, but some clarification is attempted in the following chapter.

I felt like some watcher of the skies
When a new planet swims into his ken . . .

John Keats

9

The Hyperkinetic Child — Medications

Treatment and medication are almost synonymous terms in most cultures. In Western culture, the physician has traditionally assumed the task of evaluation, diagnosis and treatment process.

There are many ethical, theoretical, practical, legal, logical and illogical complexities about the study and use, particularly the long-term use, of medications in childhood. In addition, there are medical, clinical and pharmacological perplexities due to the paradoxical responses of children to specific drugs. They do not respond in the same way as adults do to many medications. There is also a seemingly insurmountable problem caused by lack of medical agreement regarding specific diagnosis. Thus it is exceedingly difficult for parents or professionals to make meaningful comparisons of the numerous available studies of the management of hyperkinetic reaction. A familiar phrase correctly, concludes many of the now hundreds of publications on hyperkinesis: ". . . much further study is needed."

The matter of prescription drugs for hyperkinetic children reached the floor of Congress a few years ago. Concern was for possible misuse of drugs allegedly given to quiet children for "the convenience of teachers and parents." There was also question as to potential later drug abuse by such medicated children when they reached adolescence.

A federal task force was appointed in 1971 specifically to study this problem. A panel was convened by the Office of Child Development, Washington, D.C., and reviewed the findings of the federal task force. In brief, their final statement *emphasized the usefulness of medications* to treat children with hyperkinetic reactions. They concluded with a recommendation for adequate safeguards and careful medical supervision to prevent indiscriminate use of medication. No tendency toward drug abuse was found to exist in children on supervised medications.

The contention (as a theoretical possibility) that the use of long-term medications in childhood predisposes to later drug abuse has *not* been observed by this author and numerous other clinicians working with large numbers of these hyperkinetic children. The children do not "crave" the drug. They do not ask for it when discontinued. They do not feel "high" on it.

Scientific and systematic studies since 1971, involved current and retrospective evaluation of a series of adults who had been treated over a number of years for hyperkinesis during their childhood. *No* evidence was found for subsequent drug abuse.

However, in a 1970 survey of drug addicts, one subgroup studied was composed of men who were clearly Hyperkinetic during their childhood, but *untreated*. Their uncontrolled impulsivity might easily have led to drug experimentation and later abuse, which then inevitably led to physiological dependence on true addiction.

Children on medication (for that very reason), get closer attention from parent, teacher, dispensing school nurse and doctor. Through this adult contact, an attitude of responsibility develops towards the proper use of medication, with an awareness of the need for medical supervision. Children clearly differentiate between what is legitimate and illicit, by saying "it's not drugs, it's my medicine" when other children attempt to depreciate their use of a pill by teasing them.

Parents who worry about drug abuse are appropriately concerned for their child. When they finally accept the child's need for chemical controls, they are careful and responsible with the medication and watchful for side-effects. Their fears will return with each newspaper report that they feel could apply to their child. They need to discuss such concerns again and again with their doctor.

This author feels it is important for parents to be concerned about possible harm to their young, from drugs, from non-education, from disease and whatever. This is their essential child-rearing role and task. They will need informed reassurance. The physician shares their concern

135

and carefully follows current findings regarding possible ill-effects on children in general, and regularly checks their child in particular.

Occasional "medication holidays" are suggested by the author when the anxiety is very high in parents about use of medication. There must be optimum trust for a good and continuing working relationship. It is important to respect parental concern and understand that their present over-reaction may be rooted in attacks, perhaps from husband or grandparents, about damaging the child. The suggested holiday of "a month" rarely lasts more than a few days, a week at most. Parents may have forgotten the "before" state of the hyperkinetic child. Only now, after they have stopped medication, can they retrospectively realize the improvement.

Correlating the many psychopharmacological studies on children with hyperkinetic reaction is not easy. Correlation may not even be possible, due to diagnostic differences; learning disorders in some, not in others; wide variation in individual dosage needed to achieve results (from 5 mg. to 150 mg. daily), raising the question of adequate dosage of medication to effect change; and the sticky scientific issues of reliability and validity, on which one might concentrate for one hundred pages, and still be inconclusive.

With children, the age-maturational level must be considered, since serological puberty may be in process long before physical changes become evident. Such fluctuant internal changes have as yet no medical measurements for pragmatic application in clinical studies.

Observer bias is as important in the scientist as in the parent, teacher and prescribing doctor. Certain results are anticipated—for better or worse. Only computers can escape this very human quality, but alas! they are human-dependent for their programming.

So results of studies on stimulants and other drugs on children seem on the surface to be contradictory. It is important to read them at some depth to see what the actual data was. There are times when the summary does not relate to the actual data which may be so variable as to defy summary.

Drug studies also suffer from timing. A grant of money to do such studies usually prescribes "4 weeks" or "12 weeks" in its protocol. For certain of the signs rated, this is quite adequate time for assessment. But for IQ retesting and tests of perception and performance, where a child may now be "teachable" for the first time in his life, changes in learning skills cannot be expected to show significant measurable improvement until at least 12 months later.

Reports on retesting from departments of special education are beginning to reveal such improvement. However, since schools pragmatically operate on tight budgets, retesting when the child is returned to regular class is rarely as high on the priority list for the psychologists as the "crisis" disruptive child needing placement.

The "placebo" effect of the use of medication in

137

children with hyperkinetic reaction has been repeatedly studied. This placebo effect is well-known in the general field of medicine, and believed to occur with 30% of patients, no matter whether chemical or plain cornstarch is used. It is explained on the basis of renewed hope, and reassurance from a helping authority (priest, guru, physician, whatever) that change is possible. Strong suggestion (not necessarily verbalized but implied) that change will come about is also part of the placebo effect. In children with hyperkinetic reactions, excess placebo effect is not substantiated. Poor results were obtained by the use of non-specific medication (minor tranquillizers or barbiturates) where there was no improvement and the chemically paradoxical effect of hyperstimulation appeared. Hope and suggestion alone do not operate for the hyperkinetic child, his parents, teacher or physician.

Hyperkinetic reaction is based on neurophysiological dysfunctioning. These children respond to specific medications. Children with myesthenia gravis also respond to specific medication which strengthens their weakened muscles. They also need long-term, daily medication to function. There are those with bias and prejudice against "interfering with nature" who would advocate withholding specific medications from both groups.

In this culture and time, the rights of children are being reviewed and protected, from the "right to life" of the unborn to the "right to treatment" of minors with drug problems or venereal disease. The author holds that children with hyperkinetic reactions have a right to treatment. This consists of family/school/medication management, all of equal importance. The value of providing the medication now becomes the burden of responsibility of the medical profession—even of those M.D. child analysts who do not otherwise use medication in their practice. If they are not familiar or comfortable with use of drugs for hyperkinesis it is their responsibility to refer the family to a physician who is. It has been clearly shown that techniques of individual or group play therapy alone do not change the behavior of children showing hyperkinetic reactions.

A case of an 11-year-old boy, E illustrates this point quite dramatically. In 1969 the author was psychiatric consultant to the children's inpatient program of a large state hospital. On walking onto the boy's unit during the first week of arrival as consultant, E was tearing incessantly up and down the long ward corridor, jumping on and overturning chairs, touching the other children constantly on his whirlwind travels. "Who's the hyperkinetic child?" "That's a psychotic child, who's been here eight months. Nothing touches him. He's on 800 mg. Thorazine (major tranquillizer, chlorpromazine) but it makes no difference! He is still up until midnight."

The history was distressing and no tribute to the responsible professionals. The parents were seen by the author and their story follows:

E's father had been a career Army physician, and internist. He described the past 9 years as: "From the time E was 2 years, it was like living in an armed enemy camp. Nothing was safe from his attack. He was not like the 5 older children. They listened. He didn't." The mother stated that both she and her husband planned and wanted 6 children and both enjoyed and spent time with the children. Milestones were delayed for E, speech and toilet-training specifically. The disruption became unbearable. When E was 3 years old, she took him to the pediatrician on the base: "Maybe our trouble was that we knew him, he was our friend. He kept telling me he was just all boy and would outgrow it. I knew he wouldn't. I kept insisting, finally when E was 4 years old he pacified me by sending me to the base neurologist. He picked up a hearing loss in one ear, and toe-in gait which made him stumble a lot. We got orthopedic shoes which made him fall more and a hearing aid which he broke. We've had about five hearing aids since then; they do not last long."

The nursery school teacher suggested mother go to a child psychiatrist, after she had tried unsuccessfully for a week to handle him in her classroom. "We wanted the best and found a child analyst off-base. It was expensive. I took E there four mornings a week for 2½ years. The analyst did not speak to me other than telling me during the first month that E was emotionally disturbed. He was 5 years old and talking in very brief sentences when we started. I would be in the waiting room. He would be with the analyst for 10 minutes, the rest of the hour was spent running in and out of the office. I was beginning to despair. Finally, the analyst told me to bring my husband in. When he came the analyst told him he should now begin to spank the child. Also that Army life precluded security (the family had moved twice during E's life) and we should settle down as a "normal" family and spend more time with the child."

The father commented that he rarely used physical punishment for any of his children and he had found out early that it had little positive value with E. He was concerned that his anger with the boy might make him too harsh. "I started to hit him but got scared at my own anger, I didn't realize *how* mad at him I was." He decided instead to resign from service although he had only 5 years to go until he was eligible for pension. "We had spent over $20,000 on treatment for E. I had no private practice or license for this State. I had to start all over. It was hard. Things got worse. The other children started having problems, maybe we had no time left over to give them the attention they needed. We went for family therapy. Finally, the therapist asked us to leave E at home so we could talk. It was hard to get a sitter, sometimes one of us would have to stay. Most of the discussion was always E. Finally we talked about placement for E. (now 11 years old), since he had been repeatedly suspended from a special education classroom he was assigned to. Maybe he spent 30 days at school in the last three years. The school had a staffiing and suggested residential placement. That took about 8 months to happen."

Asked whether medications had been tried, father replied that the pediatrician tried phenobarbital for about 3 weeks. "That made him worse, so we stopped. We tried chloral hydrate for sleep, that didn't work." The father himself had not heard of the hyperkinetic reaction of childhood. Apparently neither had the pediatrician or child analyst involved. The parents were reliable and stable, appropriately distressed by their entire experience. They reported marked relief and a "normal" feeling at

141

home in the 8 months since E was institutionalized. They all visited monthly but reported his weekend home visits were "nightmares" due to his usual disruptive behavior.

When E was brought in from the ward his parents could not believe the change. He had come in quietly, walked over, smiled, kissed them both, sat on his father's knee and adjusted the volume on his hearing aid, telling father it was working well. He had been on dextroamphetemine 20 mg. daily for the four previous days. He had been reported asleep by 9 p.m.

This is not a "happily–ever–after" story and is not presented as such. The learning difficulties of a *non-taught* child of 11 years are great. There was an enormous amount of negative feeling for E, from his parents and all of his siblings. There was anger and self-blame at not having relevant information eight years ago. Starting all over again with E in the home was not easy, but undertaken with courage.

The road to rehabilitation for E has been hard and long and lonely. It is for him, and many other children like him, that this book was written.

As recently as the summer of 1972, the author had occasion to visit abroad and found that centers of child psychiatry in English-speaking countries are familiar with the condition and its treatment. Publications are found in the literature in England, Australia, and South Africa. However, child psychiatrists in Paris, Rome, and Lebanon did not know of the condition and requested references and available material from the author.

Despite the complexity and correlation and determination of what is and is not comparable in the literature

142

on chemotherapy for hyperkinetic reactions, it is possible to make the following summary:

Stimulant Drugs

Such stimulant drugs as dextroamphetimine (Dexedrine) and methylphenidate (Ritalin) are found to be valuable clinical tools, having a paradoxical calming effect on pre-pubertal children of both sexes.

Positive Effects

1. More controlled activity (quieter)
2. More goal-directed activity (completes tasks)
3. Fewer disruptive impulses
4. Less distractible
5. Enhanced attention and concentration
6. Better voice modulation
7. Enhanced perceptual, cognitive, performance learning
8. Better co-ordination (handwriting, drawing, gym, sports)
9. Better collaboration with family and peers
10. Personal neatness improves
11. Mood improvement: less negativistic, more pleasant, friendlier
12. Sometimes better sleep habits
13. Sometimes existing enuresis clears up.

Possible Negative Effects

1. Some appetite decrease with weight loss that stabilizes in a few weeks

2. Occasionally sleep disturbances - stays up later
3. Occasionally nail-biting or finger-picking
4. Occasionally cry more easily
5. Very rarely, may seem drowsy
6. Very rarely, circulation may become poor in hands and feet (cold)
7. Family|school may consider the medication as "the" treatment without providing needed controls and feedback
8. Severe agitation on first day, shaking, afraid (usually when child is on a diagnostic trial of medication)

The site of action in the brain of the hyperkinetic child for stimulant drugs is as yet unknown. There are a number of hypotheses, much the same as there are for the underlying cerebral pathology for the many variants of this condition.

Buckley infers a locus of amphetamine action on the ventromedial nucleus of the hypothalamus (VMH) at the base of the brain.

Wender suggested two subgroups of children with Hyperkinetic reactions: one group with defects in noradrenaline, the other group with defects in dopamine metabolism, both being neurohormones which transmit stimuli at the nerve endings in the dopamine tracts (substantia nigra to corpus striatum) of the limbic system of the brain. He proposes the caudate nucleus as the site of action of both natural dopamine and prescribed drugs effective in controlling MBD (hyperkinetic) children.

Buckley, in 1937, advanced two theories for the effec-

The reticular formation regulates our level of attention.

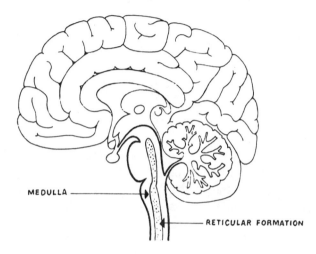

MEDULLA

RETICULAR FORMATION

Sagittal Section of the Human Brain showing the Brainstem and the Reticular Activating System.

tiveness of dextroamphetamine: (1) that it inhibited the cortex; (2) that it increased the "internal inhibitory controls" of the child, to give a calming effect by reducing disorganizationa nd confusion.

Magoum, twenty-five years later, speculated concerning the apparently contradictory sedative effect of amphetamines in children with hyperkinetic reaction. In adults they are sympathomimetic stimulants of the nervous system, giving alertness, elation, improved skill and speed.

By 1960 the *reticular activating system* (RAS) was identified at the base of the brain. A descriptive oversimplification is that the RAS is a phylogenetically old, non-specific, multineuronal, multisynaptic, relatively diffuse collection of ascending and descending pathways to convey and integrate the numerous and varied stimuli. The RAS contains complementary *excitatory* (for arousal) and *inhibitory* (for screening out and motor control) pathways. Magoum's theory postulated the RAS as the site of action for the amphetamines, which by stimulation of the *inhibitory* fibers, screened out and decreased responses to external stimuli which were not allowed to enter the cortex (conscious and purposive higher brain centers). Thus the Hyperkinetic child on stimulants could for the first time ignore the flood of stimuli and concentrate on a single task. With decreased transmission to the motor cortical areas, there was also less body movement.

A further finding in 1966, that methylphenidate (Ritalin) is an acetylcholine blocking agent, led to speculation (Ndika) that its action was by reducing active acetylcholine in the RAS (predominantly cholinergic receptors). The key to the chemical mystery is still not at hand, since it is unclear whether methylphenidate competes with and therefore inhibits acetylcholine at the neuronal end-plate receptor, or whether it blocks uptake of acetylcholine at the receptor site by depolarization.

The sleep patterns of children with hyperkinetic reaction were studied by Small, using electroencephalography to monitor the stages and total sleep time, with and without amphetamine therapy, in order to evaluate whether the quality of sleep was altered, and possibly, therefore, responsible for the improvement. He found a mild increase in sleep latency (time before falling asleep) but no change in dream or deep or total sleep periods.

Ultramicroscopic research of living tissue processes is exceedingly difficult and beseiged with experimental or post-mortem changes. Patience and repetition are essential. Findings always require duplication in other laboratories by independent and objective researchers, before scientific acceptance.

Medication dosage varies a great deal. There is no "standard" dose just as there is no "standard" hyperkinesis. With the stimulants, a child may use from 2.5 mg. to 200 mg. daily. The correct dose is that which gives optimum results with minimal undesirable side-effects. No improvement with no undesirable side-effects is an indication to increase the dosage until the clinical picture is satisfactory.

The stimulants, unlike the tranquillizers, are rapidly metabolized (within 3 to 4 hours), therefore dosage division should be arranged to cover the child's developmental and phase-related activities of school and collaborative learning of play and sports. Usually the first dose is given upon waking, then at noon and 4:00 P.M. Some children can take an 8:00 P.M. dose with no delay in falling asleep, some cannot.

Again, certain hyperkinetic children take their pill, then eat a satisfying meal. Others refuse food after their stimulant dose, so that their medication should be administered *after* the meal. Mothers usually rapidly learn the child's patterns of sleeping and eating and adjust accordingly.

The Hyperactive Child

Safer et al in 1972 reported some reduction in weight and height (in two studies) in children over 1 year on over 15 mg. of Dexedrine. This was not the case in controls or on children taking doses up to 20 mg. daily of Ritalin. The height depression was variable, whereas the suppression of weight gain was more constant. Clinically, each physician must always carefully evaluate each case for optimal benefit with minimal untoward side-effects.

Of a thousand hyperkinetic children studied, 83% responded well to Ritalin and 69% to Dexedrine, 65% to Thorazine (tranquillizer) and 57% to Mellaril (tranquillizer).

A specific amphetamine 1-amphetamine-benzedrine (Dexedrine is d-amphetamine) is not currently in wide use. Limited reporting in the literature comes from Bradley in the 1930's. He reported "levo" as half of the strength of "dextro." Arnold, Wender, et al recently studied 11 children, under a NIMH umbrella, using Benzedrine, Dexedrine, and placebo. They found the Benzedrine "slower starting" in control of hyperactivity and not significantly better than Dexedrine, but more effective than the placebo. They used too small a sample to be significant. Side effects with Benzedrine were fewer, but so too were good effects.

In puberty or adolescence, hyperkinetic children may begin to show a change in their previously good responses to amphetamines. They begin to show expectable adult responses of insomnia, marked loss of appetite and weight. The drug should be stopped. Some clinicians find an abrupt discontinuation no problem. Others prefer to taper over two to three weeks.

Some hyperkinetic children (about 30%) show enough inner controls and growth to function without further medication or psychotherapy. Another third remain hyperkinetic—on a larger scale! These children continue to require the gamut of assistance described above, namely from family and school, often within a larger social network, which may need to include the high school counsellor and, if there is a clash with the law, the juvenile officer.

Medication may still be mandatory to decrease restlessness and impulsive activity and increase attention. The tricyclic amines or tranquillizers discussed in the next sections should be given individual clinical trial.

Usually the hyperkinetic child remains on amphetamines from about the age of 6 until he is 12 years old. Some "graduate" earlier, others later. It is indeed a long journey to self-control and social adaptation, for child and family alike.

Caffeine

A recent interesting study is reported by Schnackenberg, who substituted caffeine for methylphenidate (Ritalin) in eleven children who were on the latter medication for their hyperkinetic symptoms. The author remarks that his results with two cups of coffee (equivalent to 200–300 mg. caffeine) per day were as satisfactory as the amphetamines, at one tenth of the cost. Careful

The Hyperactive Child

double-blind studies were suggested with attempts to match specific hyperkinetic subgroups with specific medication regimens.

Antidepressants

Antidepressants were discovered in the 1940s almost fortuitously from noting the euphoriant effects of certain anti-tuberculosis medications, which were monoamine oxidase (brain enzyme) inhibitors. Some serious side effects resulted in temporary U.S.F.D.A. suspension. They are again in limited use, not in children. The tricyclic amine antidepressants were perfected in the 1950's.

Since stimulants are very short-acting mood elevators, it was not long before antidepressants (longer-acting mood elevators) were given clinical trials with hyperkinetic children.

The tricyclic amines are in wide usage for adults. There are a few clinical studies recently comparing their effectiveness with tranquillizers, in children with hyperkinetic reactions.

The Schilder "catecholamine theory" postulates that in adults in depression the brain's total production of monoamine is lowered, and in mania it is elevated. Wender et al, in 1971 studied a small group of hyperkinetic children, to measure urinary monoamine metabolites for 24-hour periods. The 9 hyperkinetic children showed no differences from the 6 controls.

In adults, the tricyclic amine antidepressants are believed to exert their therapeutic effect by elevating cerebral catecholamines. It is uncertain how they work in

150

hyperkinetic children, but Huessy and Wright, in 1970, reported a clinical study of 52 hyperkinetic children given average single doses of 50 mg. imipramine (Tofranil) daily. Sixty-seven percent showed marked improvement, with no undesirable side-effects clinically or on extensive laboratory tests.

Since the tricyclic antidepressant Tofranil has for many years been used to assist nocturnal bedwetting, it is considered clinically safe for children. There are no reports in the literature of untoward side-effects. On trial some parents will report no change in the hyperkinesis. Occasionally, in an adolescent newly on trial or on changeover at puberty from amphetamine, drowsiness for the first few days may be reported. Giving the total dose in the evening will usually control daytime drowsiness. Unlike the amphetamines, which are excreted within hours in the urine, the tricyclic amines take about 20 hours or longer to be metabolized, therefore are longer acting.

Sedatives

Sedatives act by generalized depression of the cortex of the adult brain in moderate doses. In the hyperkinetic child, the most commonly used medium-acting barbiturate, phenobarbital, is a paradoxical stimulant. The child becomes hyperexcitable by day and very restless at night. Increasing the dosage gives ataxia, (gait incoordination) and drowsiness before any control of hyperkinesis. It is contraindicated in hyperkinetic children, unless there is co-existing epilepsy, uncontrollable by other medications.

The Hyperactive Child

Tranquillizers

There are literally dozens of tranquillizers on the market, divided into groups called major and minor, with numerous subgroups classified by chemical structure. Only the two major tranquillizers most widely in use with hyperkinetic children will be discussed: thioridazine (Mellaril) and chlorpromazine (Thorazine). Both are of the phenothiazine subgroup, discovered in the late 1940s, the latter in France.

This group of medications has changed the entire management of emotional and behavioral problems by quietening even persons with agitation so profound that they lose reality contact. With administration of phenothiazines, disturbed persons become calmer and even return to acceptable functioning. Many patients who had been in state institution for countless years improved with these medications and were released. These tranquillizers have also been dubbed "anti-psychotic" drugs.

From the early 1940s, Lauretta Bender courageously studied severely disturbed children, using drug trials to mitigate the drastic disruptive and self-mutilatory behavior of some children with severe organic brain damage. Out of this pioneering work grew other studies. Finally numerous clinical observations accumulated about the effects of phenothiazines on hyperkinetic children. Also comparisons of phenothiazine, amphetamines and other drugs were done.

Millichamp reports closely similar improvement with

thioridazine (Mellaril)—57% and chlorpromazine (Thorazine)—55% improvement.

Negative Effects

Possible undesirable effects of the tranquillizing phenothiazines are:

1. Some daytime drowsiness, often clearing by the second week (more likely with Thorazine).
2. More behavioral and social than learning improvement.
3. Some weight gain and ravenous appetite (which may result in social effects like being teased for obesity).
4. Rarely (1% of cases) bedwetting or even daytime dribbling (cholinergic bladder fibers possibly affected). Mellaril is more likely to do this.
5. Very rarely, lowered blood count, which is an indication to stop the drug.
6. Rarely, tremors or incoordinated movements with very high doses.

A simple switch from one to the other phenothiazine may be effective. Reduction of dosage may be tried. If this does not assist, a trial of Tofranil (see previous section), Benadryl, or Vistaril (see next section) might be attempted. Sometimes return to a previously effective amphetamine is worthwhile (from the author's experience this has at times been effective).

The site of action of the phenothiazines is still unknown, but thought to be similar to that of amphetamines, namely the Reticular Activating System (RAS) but by inhibitory effect on its arousal component. Another theory is by reduction of available cerebral catecholamines.

Antihistamines

These "anti-allergy" drugs were the precursors of the phenothiazines in the early 1940s. They were found useful to reduce nausea and vomiting and reverse the skin reaction in various food and contact allergies. Their undesirable side-effect was sedation. Since they were found to be exceptionally safe chemicals, the antihistamines Benadryl (diphenhydramine hydrochloride), Vistaril (hydroxyzine hydrochloride), and Phenergan (promethazine hydrochloride) became widely used in pediatric practice, easily dispensed as flavored syrups and elixirs. The sedative effect was exploited in assisting sick, frightened babies, infants, and children in pain. They are particularly safe and helpful as nighttime sedatives in those who require separation from parents for hospitalization.

Vistaril and Benadryl have been used in some hyperkinetic children: those refractory to other drugs more commonly used, and those with a history of allergies. The required dose may vary from 50 mg. to 200 mg. daily.

Other Drugs

Fish and Bender discuss other drugs in detail, including:

Chlordiazepoxide (Librium)

Studied also by Zrull, this drug may be helpful where the hyperkinetic child is non-responsive to the stimulants or phenothiazines.

Lithium Carbonate

The use of lithium carbonate in psychotic hyperactive children is reported in Scandinavian literature, in dosages up to 600 mg. daily. A few cases were children of a manic-depressive parent. This evokes interesting possibilities for genetic research and possible differentiation of a "sub-type" if the overactivity of the child can be chromosomally linked to that of the parent. Whitehead in the U.S., in 1970, found lithium carbonate to have no more than placebo effect on seven hyperkinetic children to whom it was administered.

Dilantin (Diphenylhydantoin)

This is a good anti-seizure medication that should be used only with caution, and when indicated. Caution is specifically emphasized because the use of this drug was popularized by the lay press within this decade as a general panacea for obsessive thoughts, impulsive behavior, general unhappiness, anxiety, and a number of assorted discomforts. Dilantin may *not* be used with impunity. Like all of the other medications mentioned here, it should not be used when the child is not under care of a physician. Side-effects are rare, but can be kept to a minimum with competent medical surveillance. Indiscriminate use of any chemical agent is to be deplored—in adult and child alike.

Lack of diagnostic agreement and underdiagnosis is often due to the fact that the physician sees the child for about five minutes, usually with three adults, himself, nurse and mother in the room. Such artificial control requires supplemental history from two other arenas: home and school. The mother and teacher are essential informants. They spend exhausting hours watching and being worn down by the ceaseless, unproductive, heedless activity. They have no illusions that this child is a "normal" variant. They can perceive him as a lonely, spinning satellite who only makes contact with his world by collision. These impacts are frequent and accelerate with the slightest stress.

What Medication Cannot Do

Medication cannot 1. compensate for "lost" years of learning, not only academic, but practical tasks like skill at play, dressing, chores, games, table manners, etc. Patient and gentle re-teaching should be done as soon as the child settles down on medication. Many of the skills can be learned with encouragement and persistence. Skills in appropriate social behavior with peers should be remembered as being of equal importance as behavior toward adults.

Neither can medication provide discipline. Chapter V explores the ongoing constant daily feedback from parent to child needed for effective mutual respect in achieving acceptable behavior. A pill is no shortcut.

Without other changes, medication cannot improve self-esteem. The child will need to see himself in an altered light, when his behavior and general performance have improved. He will need recognition, repeated reassurance that he is good (whenever he is). Slowly, with testing, he will begin to develop internal assurance and self-confidence.

Medication cannot provide love. In a child-rejecting family, the most a parent can give the child may be a pill and material necessities. In extreme cases, where a scapegoat is essential to the family disequilibrium, even the needed pills may be withheld, to "prove" that the child is "bad". No chemical can repair such destructive interaction. Intensive family therapy will be needed.

Medication cannot reverse essential deficits such as cerebral palsy, mental retardation, speech disorders, specific learning difficulties in reading, writing, or mathematics. These will all require assistance by use of special education techniques—physical or speech therapy, kinesthetic reinforcement learning approaches, and more sophisticated newly-developed rapid feedback, audio visual aids and "teaching machines".

157

The true heroism is patience

Robert Louis Stevenson

10

The Hyperkinetic Child — Prognosis and Prevention

The outlook for the future of a specific child with problems is frequently a haunting question to the parent who lives day by day, to the teacher who tries to plan for ongoing education, and also to the pediatrician or family doctor who has concern about how long before the problem clears up.

For some parents, this search for an answer about the future becomes an obsession, as they try doctor after doctor, clinic after clinic, test after test. These tests indicate the current state of the child, while the search is really for an answer to questions about the future: "What is the prognosis?" "Will he be self-sufficient?" "Will he complete high school?" "Will he be able to go to college?" "Will he be a hyperkinetic adult?" "Will he be able to get married?" "Will his children be the same?" "Will other children we have be the same?" "Will he need medication all his life?" "Will he end up in jail?" "Will he end up in an institution?" These and many more are the unanswered questions for a child with hyperkinetic reaction.

The essence of good public health is good prevention. Toward this aim scientific medicine has launched intensive studies of specific diseases to search for a causative factor, which then may be studied in detail, so that its effect in the community may be predicted with precision. Certain parasitic diseases have yielded well to such research, and prognosis for certain diseases such as malaria and bilharzia is known. They may be brought under complete control, if there is a great deal of effort and expenditure upon the known sources and risks of human infection by the parasite. Breakdown of protective barriers is due only to human error or inadequate control efforts.

Epidemics of bacterial infections which are well-known to medicine, such as typhoid, tuberculosis, or smallpox, occur under conditions where they are predictable, such as in disaster areas with intense crowding, after floods or earthquakes, with intense malnutrition. Bringing relief and specific medication within a reasonable time can halt the epidemic, reduce the mortality, and the infection can again be brought under strict control.

However, with a clinical "syndrome", which is a collection of similar but not identical problems making up a clearly recognized clinical picture, there are no neat stages like the life cycle of the malaria parasite in the mosquito and in the blood of man.

There are three ways in which the outlook for children with hyperkinetic reaction may be approached:

1. clinical impression of those who work for many years with great numbers of these children, such as clinics, pediatricians or psychiatrists, relying upon their medical observations and reports without detailed, objective data, and controlled studies.

2. careful longitudinal follow-up studies of large numbers of children with the same diagnostic category, objective comparisons, adequate controls, carefully checked for validity and reliability.

3. retrospective studies in later years of persons believed to have had in their youth the clinical syndrome of hyperkinetic reaction.

All three of these methods are easy to discredit as far as scientific accuracy goes. However, most parents and teachers are not intensely interested in scientific accuracy, since to them their particular child is 100% of the question they are asking, whereas to the statistics he may be one out of 500. However, having some knowledge of how great numbers of hyperkinetic children progress usually gives the parents hope, direction, and encouragement to carry on. To the child-rejecting family, however, negative statistics may be grasped as one further documentation that extended effort with this particular child is valueless. They fit such information into their frame of reference that the child is "bad" and "hopeless" and therefore should be institutionalized and the burden of rearing given to "the state" or to strangers in foster homes.

Prognosis

There are some general prognostic indicators which hold true for almost any problem of child or adult, in that if these variables are measured, they make for a predictably favorable or poor outcome. These are:

1. satisfactory school performance (average or above-average I.Q.)
2. acceptable social adjustment with an intact family
3. appropriate emotional development and adjustment

All of these three factors should be looked at separately from the Hyperactive motor behavior, the distractibility, the impulsivity, and the socio-economic status, to see on which side of the scale they are to be weighed in predicting the long-term outcome. Consistent family cooperativeness, reliable maintenance of educational, socialization, and medication programs to assist the child all count in his favor.

If there is some degree of mental retardation in addition to the hyperkinetic reaction, the outlook will be less favorable for attainment of unassisted independence in adult life. Broken families with prolonged stress of an unstable domestic and school situation will make for additional emotional problems. Learning disabilities superimposed upon the hyperkinetic behavior will predictably impair progress, although not necessarily arrest it. The presence of unacceptable or anti-social behavior with a history of recurrent stealing, fire-setting, or recurrent physical aggression or violence would also undisputedly make for a difficult future adjustment, particularly if compounded with some degree of intellectual deficiency. Again, the factor of severe emotional disturbance such as presence of psychosis would add still further stress to the system, particularly if in addition there were other problems such as broken home, or severe learning difficulties.

Clinical Impression

Most neurologists and psychiatrists as well as pediatricians who work long-term with hyperkinetic children have a clinical impression that these children do indeed improve, that the excessive motor movement and the impulsivity are substantially mitigated by puberty.

This author shares the impression of optimism. In 10 years of direct follow-up with 78 assorted children with hyperkinetic reaction, the author has already graduated 15% of them at puberty without the need for further medication. For the first two years of puberty, 5% of the children have required the use of phenothiazines (when the stimulants were no longer effective). The rest of the children are still currently under the age of 12 years. They are being seen in monthly follow-up medication groups with their parents.

The author's impression is also that with good special education techniques there is improvement in learning, and interesting "breakthrough" periods with spurts of spontaneous learning which will surprise and please both parents and teachers. There are also similar peaks of improved co-ordination performance, particularly where there has been repeated and patient effort to assist the child with basic simple skills such as throwing and catching a ball, or balancing on skates. When mastery is achieved in a small area, there will be a sudden generalization of this skill to broader areas such as capacity to collaborate in neighborhood ball games and ice hockey games. Improvement in self-esteem usually goes along with such progress, as well as signs of maturity and independence both at home and in the classroom. These changes have been noted even in a few homes with child rejection, where the improvement has made for some acceptance and improved interaction between parent and child.

Continuing the author's subjective impression is the observation that the hyperkinetic child's impulsivity, tendency to distractibility, and some perceptual difficulties tend to remain but are not insurmountable. These are special children, and need special personal investment and understanding.

Physicians who have had a great deal of experience in this field are Bradley, who states that on informal clinical reports of over 500 hyperkinetic children there is a decrease in hyperactivity with maturation; Laufer and Denhoff, who also state that the hyperactivity tends to disappear between ages 12 and 18.

Longitudinal Follow-up Studies

Good prospective or anterospective studies are just beginning to appear in the literature. It is important to remember that the recognition of the condition of hyperkinetic reaction of childhood was dignified to a diagnostic category for the first time in the DSM II in 1968.

Weiss and co-workers from McGill University, Montreal, Canada, did a 5-year follow-up on 64 severely handicapped hyperkinetic children between the ages of 6 and 13, and reported their findings in 1969. It is a careful, well-documented study of very disturbed children, attempting cross-validation measures with control groups, and is a good scientific work, despite the enormous logistical difficulties of such long-term follow-up studies. Behavior, social adaptation, academic function, cognitive and motor function, all improved. Only 10% of the families received family or individual psychotherapy. Although there was a high frequency of academic retardation in these children, only 15% were able to receive remedial education additional to regular schooling, due to an absence of such remedial educational facilities in the area. The findings therefore must be scrutinized in this context.

Retrospective Studies

These are much easier to find in the literature, and are of value, although again, they may be criticized regarding the accuracy of the diagnosis, since, as previously mentioned, the syndrome has so recently been defined, and contains such a heterogeneous group of children.

A much quoted study is that of Menkes at Johns Hopkins, who did a 25-year follow-up of 14 children diagnosed as "Minimal Brain Dysfunction". Eleven of the patients were examined; 8 still had definite abnormalities on neurological examination, 3 were reported as "still restless", 2 were retarded and institutionalized, 8 were self-supporting, and most of the subjects reported that between the ages of 8 and 21 the hyperactivity had "disappeared". He found that low IQ correlated with an inability to achieve social self-sufficiency.

Another retrospective study was done by Robbins at Saint Louis. Between 1924 and 1929, 524 children were seen by the juvenile court for anti-social behavior. They were followed up 30 years later. Forty-five per cent of these children, on retrospective scrutiny were thought to have diagnosis of hyperkinetic behavior. The study, however, seems more directed at delinquent behavior than motor activity and educational achievement. The delinquency in these children, (as in many other studies of delinquents) correlated with disrupted homes rather than with low socio-economic class.

The Adolescent Clinic at University of Washington provided Hammar with 73 children retrospectively diagnosed as hyperkinetic, whom he found to be underachieving adolescents with persistent school problems. He drew the conclusion that while the hyperactivity had settled in most of the subjects, their psychological problems had persisted, but had changed their form from hyperactive motor behavior into sociopathy and a tendency toward emotional instability. Percentage breakdown is not clear, nor the diagnostic criteria which he used.

Shelley and Riester attempted to follow the hyperkinetic syndrome from childhood to adulthood in a retrospective study done at an Air Force training base, using 16 cases—14 males and 2 females—of previously undiagnosed "minimal brain damage," between the ages of 18 to 23, who were referred to a psychiatrist because of difficulty in coping with the basic requirements of military training. From the psychiatric evaluation, neurological evaluation, and psychological testing, 12 of the 16 studied had a childhood history compatible with hyperkinetic reaction. This had tended to disappear by the onset of adolescence, without any medication. Twelve of the 16 had school problems; however *all of the 16 had graduated from high school*. Ten of them had a history of speech problems, which also seemed to disappear with age, and only 3 of the 16 showed persistent speech disturbance at clinical examination. None of them had difficulty collaborating with peers at the Air Force Base, none had serious psychiatric maladjustments, and all seemed to cope fairly well with their life tasks prior to Air Force entry. All of the 16 men studied seemed to have retained minor perceptual-motor defects which prevented optimal performance and resulted in their referral to the Department of Psychiatry for evaluation.

In conclusion, the reader is left still uncertain about the future for a specific child with hyperkinetic reaction.

The Hyperactive Child

These diverse studies indeed reflect the current state of essential inability to predict with any accuracy. When experts disagree on incidence and diagnosis, how can they agree on prognosis?

The problem of diagnostic heterogeneity is one of the most important issued in this type of research. A possible solution is to subdivide the patients into more homogeneous clusters, according to behavioral profile, by using cluster analysis computer programming. This classification could then show that some groups change in one function while others may not. Some may show drug effects, but in entirely different areas, in a range from motor activity to school achievement. Definite subgroups could perhaps be defined who respond differentially to the various treatment programs.

In general, however, this author feels that the outlook for hyperkinetic children is optimistic, given an intense and consistent total program to meet their emotional, social, educational and medical needs. Parents and teachers need to be given optimum support, encouragement, and consultation throughout the stormy school years, so that they may continue to engage with, to educate, to guide toward independence and self-sufficiency, these hyperkinetic children with their "built-in dynamos".

Prevention

The issue of *prevention* is almost impossible to discuss when so little is of certainty as to "a specific cause." Where so many factors are potential causes, a discussion of prevention of hyperkinetic reactions of childhood is no more meaningful than being for motherhood or the flag.

Primary prevention could include good ante-natal care for the mother; avoidance of medication or malnutrition during pregnancy; avoidance of unnecessary induction of labor, optimum delivery techniques for the infant; optimum maturity of the fetus; optimum neonatal care and oxygenation; adequate neonatal and infancy nutrition; prevention of encephalitis and head injury—in short, good sensible health care.

In spite of having none of the problems possibly related to "minimal brain dysfunction", some children still appear with hyperkinetic reaction in childhood. Prevention at that point is directed secondarily toward *reduction of complications* such as school difficulties, social difficulties, and interpersonal emotional effects such as low self-esteem, sense of failure, and rejection by the parents.

Such secondary prevention essentially takes the form of a total "network" of treatment. This should start first with a screening program at the preschool or kindergarten level to identify possible cases, and then follow up with a complete medical work-up, including a neurological and psychological examination to provide as valuable a profile as possible to enable educators to map out an individual course of special education for the specific child. For the diagnosed hyperkinetic child, adequate medication is essentially preventative of additional learning and emotional problems. When the child is desk-ready and able to

171

The Hyperactive Child

sit in a classroom without disrupting it, special education forms the main emphasis of treatment together with all of the secondary benefits entailed in schooling, such as peer relations, socialization, general collaboration, phase-related activities at all other levels including recreation and sports activities.

The adults should always remember (even in periods of ultimate exasperation) that for the hyperkinetic child, as for them, the road is long and lonely, rugged and really frightening. He needs not only a hand, but a continuous handrail over the bumpy stretches, so that in the end he may walk alone, comfortably, with hard-earned self-confidence.

*You cannot prevent the birds of
sorrow from flying over your head,
But you can prevent them from building
nests in your hair.*

Chinese Proverb

11

Epilogue

Hyperkinetic reaction of childhood is a great masquerader, so that careful evaluation is needed to prevent overdiagnosis. "All that wriggles" is not necessarily a hyperkinetic child. With skill and patience hyperanxious and hyperaggressive children can be identified for specific management. Normal hyperactivity that is phase-related is predictable and should be recognized, so that informed reassurance can be given to those seeking clarification.

Here are some of the labels tagged to children brought for evaluation: cranky, stubborn, dumb, deaf, mean, spiteful, vicious, jealous, impossible, disruptive, unruly, monster, aggressive, high energy, hyper, tornado, top, machine, underachiever, retard, devil-angel, animal, con-artist, puzzle, bored, too intelligent, just-a-boy, noisy, nervous, athletic.

If the diagnosis confirms that there is hyperkinetic reaction then it should be understood that the real cause is essentially beyond control of the child. It is within his brain, possibly neurochemical in nature and at specific diencephalic sites. At this stage, no autopsy studies are available for confirmation. In the absence of histological cerebral lesions, the behavioristically descriptive title of hyperkinetic reaction of childhood is preferable to others that imply specific pathology in the brain.

A definite cluster of signs and symptoms make this condition rapidly recognizable. Screening programs at preschool or kindergarten level are needed to identify the thousands of little ones at high risk and who need further evaluation and work-up for definitive diagnosis and treatment planning. An approach of concerned, informed common sense works best. Screening for hyperkinetic children is as important a public health task as screening for tuberculosis or diabetes mellitus or any other handicap.

While it is not yet preventable, hyperkinetic reaction of childhood is eminently treatable. The outlook contains hope for improvement, given an optimum collaborative family, school, and medical network. If the basic endowments of the child include a normal intellect, his chances for good adult adjustment are favorable.

When the family, social and intellectual structures are fragmented, the problems for the hyperkinetic child are augmented. The task of "life-engineering" at a given point in time may be overwhelming for child and helpers alike. Nonetheless, whatever small helps can be offered should be given in the interest of possible later changes.

The most important resources in any community are its schools. For the hyperkinetic child, the most important resource is the availability of special education facilities that can provide more structure, less stimulation, and specialized help with specific learning difficulties. Communities could give priority to expenditure for screening and special education programs to assist the 5-10% of elementary school children who are in need of this kind of service.

It is good judgment to provide adequate education and training today to attempt to prevent social dependency in the future. Throughout the management of hyperkinetic children there must be consistent expectation of acceptable behavior and standards. Positive recognition for effort rather than constant negative attacks from authority figures finally achieves better results.

Knowledgeable professionals able to function comfortably together with close interdisciplinary co-operation form the core of workers diagnosing, treating, and above all, researching this riddle. Neurologists, pediatricians, family physicians, psychiatrists, researchers, teachers, parents, all share an ultimate goal of cure and prevention of the hyperkinetic syndrome and all its variants. Man's unique strength is in the ability to grow in the face of difficulties and to overcome rather than despair.

Optimism? Determination? How else was Science born of man?

177

Bibliography

Anderson, C., and Plymate, H. B. "Management of the Brain-damaged Adolescent." *American Journal of Orthopsychiatry*, 32 (1960): 492–500.

Annell, A. L. "Lithium in the treatment of children and adolescents." *Acta Psychiatrica Scandinavica*, Suppl., 207 (1969): 19–30.

Arnold, L. E. et al. "Levoamphetamine and Dextroamphetamine: comparative Efficacy in the Hyperkinetic Syndrome". *Archives of General Psychiatry*, 27: (December 1972) 816–822.

Bender, L. "Psychological Problems of Children with Organic Brain Disease" *American Journal of orthopsychiatry*, 19 (1949): 404–415.

_____ "Chemotherapy is Child Psychiatry" *New York State Medical Journal*, 56(1956):2791–95.

Blau, A. "Mental Changes Following Head Trauma in

Children" *Archives of Neurology and Psychiatry*, 35 (1937): 723–769.

Bond, E. D. and Appel, L. E. "The Treatment of Behavior Disorders Following Encephalitis" New York: *Commonwealth Fund, Division of Publications*, 1931.

———— "Postencephalitic, Ordinary and Extra-ordinary Children" *Journal of Pediatrics*, 1 (1932): 310–314.

———— and Smith, L. H. "Postencephalitic Behavior Disorders: A ten-year review of the Franklin School." *American Journal of Psychiatry*, 92 (1935): 17–33.

Bradley, C. "The Behavior of Children receiving Benzedrine." *American Journal of Psychiatry*, 94 (1937): 577–585.

———— "Benzedrine and Dexedrine in the Treatment of Children's Behavior Disorders." *Pediatrics*, 5 (1950): 24–36.

Broderick, C. B. "Children's Romances" *Sexual Behavior*, 2 (May, 1972): 15.

Burks, H. F. "Effects of Amphetamine Therapy on Hyperkinetic Children." *Archives of General Psychiatry*, 11 (1964): 604–609.

Cantwell, D. P. "Psychiatric Illness in the Families of Hyperactive Children" *Archives of General Psychiatry*, 27 (Sepetmber, 1972): 414–417.

Chess, S. "Diagnosis and Treatment of the Hyperactive Child." *New York Journal of Medicine*, 60, (1959): 2379–2385.

Clements, S. D. "Minimal Brain Dysfunction in Children" *NINDB Monograph* 3: Public Health Service, 1966: 1415.

_____ and Peters, J. E. "Minimal Brain Dysfunctions in the School Age Child." *Archives of General Psychiatry*, 6 (1962): 185–197.

Conners, C. K. "The Syndrome of Minimal Brain Dysfunction: Psychological Aspects", *Pediatric Clinics of North America*, 14, (1967): 749–766.

_____ Eisenberg, L. and Barcai, A. "Effect of Dextroamphetamine on Children." *Archives of General Psychiatry*, 17 (1967): 478–485.

Cytryn, L., Gilbert, A., and Eisenberg, L. "The Effectiveness of Tranquilizing Drugs plus Supportive Psychotherapy in Treating Behavior Disorders of Children." A double-blind study of 80 out-patients. *American Journal of Orthopsychiatry*, 30 (1960): 113–128.

David, O., Clark, J., Voeller, K. "Lead and Hyperactivity," *The Lancet*, 2 (October 28, 1972): 900–3.

DiMascio A. "Psychopharmacology in Children", *Massachusetts Institute of Mental Health*, Volume 1 (Fall, 1970).

Eisenberg, E. "Dynamic Considerations Underlying the Management of The Brain-Damaged Child" *General Practitioner*, 14 (1956): 101–106.

_____ "Management of the Hyperkinetic Child" *Developmental Medicine and Child Neurology*, 5 (1966): 593–598.

_____ "Principles of Drug Therapy in Child Psychiatry with Special Reference to Stimulant Drugs", *American Journal of Orthopsychiatry*, 41 (1971): 371–379.

_____ and Talbot, Kagan. "Psychopharmacology in

Childhood", Chapter 9, *Behavioral Science in Pediatric Medicine*. Philadelphia: W. B. Saunders Company, 1971.

Epstein, L. C., Lasagna, L., Conners, C. I., and Rodriguez, A. "Correlation of Dextroamphetamine Excretion and Drug Response in Hyperkinetic Children." *Journal of Nervous and Mental Disorders*, 146 (1968): 136–146.

Fischer K. C. and Wilson, W. P. "Methylphenidate and the Hyperkinetic State", *Diseases of the Nervous System*, 32 (October, 1971): 10, 695–698.

Fish, B. "Drug Use in Psychiatric Disorders of Children" *American Journal of Psychiatry*, February Supplement (1968): 124:31–36.

_____"The 'One Child One Drug' myth of Stimulants in Hyperkinesis" *Archives of General Psychiatry*, Volume 25, (September 1971), 193–203.

Greenberg, L. M. et al. "Effects of Dextroamphetramine, Chlorpromazine and Hydroxyzine on Behavioral Performances in Hyperactive Children" *American Journal of Psychiatry*, 129:5, (November, 1972): 532–540.

Gross, M. D. and Wilson, W. C. "Treatment of Minimal Brain Dysfunction in Childhood", *Current Psychiatric Therapies*, (1967).

Hammar, S. L. "School underachievement in the Adolescent: a review of 73 cases." *Pediatrics*, 40 (1967): 373–381.

Hohman, L. B. "Post-Encephalitic Behavior Disorders in Children" *John Hopkins Hospital Bulletin*, 380 (1922): 372–375.

Huessy, H. R. and Wright, A. L. "The effect of

Imipramine on Hyperkinetic Children" *Acta Paedop-sychiatrica* 37 (1970): 7–8, 194–199.

Hutt, S. J. and Hutt, C. "Hyperactivity in a group of Epi-leptic (and some non-epileptic brain-damaged children)" *Epilepsies* 5 (1964): 334.

Knobel, M. "Psychopharmacology for the Hyperkinetic Child." *Archives of General Psychiatry* 6 (1962): 198–202.

_____Wolman, M. B., and Mason, E. "Hyperkinesis and organicity in Children" *Archives of General Psychia-try*, 1 (1958): 310–321.

Krakowski, A. J. "Amitriptyline in Treatment of Hyperkinetic Children: A double blind study." *Psy-chosomatics*, 6 (1965): 355–360.

Magoum H. W. *The Waking Brain*, 2nd Edition, Springfield, Illinois: Charles Thomas, 1963.

Menkes, M., Rowe, J. S., and Menkes, J. H. "A twenty-five-year Follow-up Study on the Hyperkinetic Child with Minimal Brain Dysfunction". *Pediatrics*, 39 (1967): 393–399.

Millichamp, J. G., and Boldrey, E. E. "Studies in Hyperkinetic Behavior" *Neurology* Volume 17 (May 1967): 467–471.

_____.and Fowler, G. W."Treatment of 'Minimal Brain Dysfunction' Syndromes" *Pediatric Clinics of North America*, 14 (1967): 767–777.

Montagu, A. *Prenatal Influences*, Springfield, Illinois: Charles Thomas, 1962.

Montgomery County, Maryland Board of Education "Project Focus" *report.* Unpublished manuscript. (In-cidence 22% "attention span" problems)

The Hyperactive Child

Morris, H. H. Jr., Escoll, P. J., Wexler, R., "Aggressive Behavior Disorders of Childhood" a follow-up study. *American Journal of Psychiatry*, 112 (1956): 991–997.

Ndika, L. I. "Methylphemidate Effect on Neuromuscular Transmittion," *Archives of Internationales Pharmacodynamie et de Therapie*, 163 (1966): 103–109.

Olds, J., Milner, P. "Self-stimulation of the Brain" *Science*, 127 (1958): 315–324.

_____ "Positive Reinforcement Produced by Electrical Stimulation of Septal Area and Other Regions of Rat Brain" *Journal of Comprehensive Physiology and Psychology*, 47 (1954): 419–427.

Paine, R. S., Werry, J. S., Quay, H. C. "A Study of Minimal Cerebral Dysfunction" *Developmental Medicine and Child Neurology* 10: (1968): 505–520.

Prechtl, H. F. R., Stemmer, C. J. "The Choreiform Syndrome in Children" *Developmental Medicine and Child Neurology*, 4 (1962): 119–127.

Renshaw, Domeena C., "Psychiatric consultation to a Department of Special Education" *Woman Physician*, September, 1972.

_____ "How Can Teachers Cope with Stealing in the Classroom?" *Journal of School Health*, September, 1972.

_____ "When to Refer a Child to Special Education", *Pointer*, Spring, (1972).

_____ "Teacher as Healer of the Disturbed Child", *Pointer* (Winter, 1972.): 140–145.

_____ "Sexuality in Children", *The Medical Aspects of Human Sexuality*, (October, 1971.)

Robins, L. *Deviant Children Grown Up*, Baltimore: William and Wilkins, 1966.

Routtenberg, A. "The Two-Arousal Hypothesis: Reticular Formation and Limbic System", *Psychology Review*, 75 (1968): 51–80.

Safer, D. et al. "Depression of Growth in Children on Stimulant Drugs" *New England Journal of Medicine*, 287:5, (August 3, 1972): 217–220.

Schaefer, E. S., Bayley, N. "Maternal Behavior, Child Behavior and Their Intercorrelations from Infancy Through Adolescence". Monograph. *Society for Research in Child Development*, 28 (1963): No. 3, 87.

Schnackenberg, R. C. "Caffeine as a Substitute for Schedule II Stimulants in Hyperkinetic Children", *American Journal of Psychiatry*, 130:7, 796–798, July 1973.

Shelley, E. M. & Riester, A. "Syndrome of Minimal Brain Damage in Young Adults" *Diseases of the Nervous System*, (May 1972).

Shirley, M. "A Behavior Syndrome Characterizing Prematurely Born Children" *Child Development* 10 (1939): 2.

Small, A, Hibi S., Feinberg, I. "Effects of Dextroamphetamine on EEG Sleep Patterns of Hyperactive Children" *Archives of General Psychiatry*, Volume 25, (October, 1971): 369–379.

Stewart, M., Ferris, A., Pitts, N., Jr., Craig, A. G. "The Hyperactive Child Syndrome" *American Journal of Orthopsychiatry* 36 (1966): 861–867.

Strauss, A. A., Kephart, N. C. "Psychopathology and Education of the Brain-Injured Child" *Progress in Theory and Clinic*, Volume II. New York: Grune & Stratton, 1955.

Thomas, A., Chess, S., and Birch, H. G. *Temperament and Behavior Disorders in Children* New York: New York University Press, (1968)

Towbin, A., "Cerebral Hypoxic Damage in Fetus and Newborn" *Archives of Neurology* 20 (1969): 35–43.

_____ "Organic Causes of Minimal Brain Dysfunction" *Journal of the American Medical Association*, Volume 217:9, (August, 1971): 1207–1214.

Weiss, G. et al. "Studies on the Hyperactive Child", Five Year Follow-up. *Archives of General Psychiatry*, Volume 24, (May, 1971): 409–414.

Wender, P. H. *Minimal Brain Dysfunction in Children* New York: Wiley-Interscience, 1971.

Whitehead, P. L., Clark, L. D., "Effect of Lithium Carbonate, Placebo, and Thioridazine on Hyperactive Children" *American Journal of Psychiatry*, 127:6, :1970): 824–825.

Winsberg, B. E. et al. "Effects of Imipramine and Dextroamphetamine on Behavior of Neuropsychiatrically Impaired Children" *American Journal of Psychiatry* 128:11 (May, 1972): 1425–31.

Woody, R. H. "Electroencephalography and Minimal Cerebral Dysfunction: A research-based stance for School Health Personnel" *Journal of School Health*, (September, 1971): 351–354.

Zeilberger, J., Sampen, S. E., and Sloan, H. N. "Modification of A Child's Problem Behaviors in the Home with the Mother as a Therapist" *Journal of Applied Behavioral Analysis*, 1: (1958): 47–53.

Zrull, J. P., Westman, J. C., Arthur, B., Bell, W. A. "A Comparison of Chlordiazepoxide, d-amphetamine and Placebo in the Treatment of the Hyperkinetic Syndrome in Children" *American Journal of Psychiatry* (1963): 120:590–591.

Zrull, J. P., Westman, J. C., Arthur, B., and Rice, D. L. "An Evaluation of Methodology used in the Study of Psychoactive Drugs for Children" *Journal of American Academic Child Psychiatry* 5 (1966): 284–291.

INDEX

Academic problems, 114
Acetylcholine, 101, 146
Acting out, 113
Action, 77
Addington, J., 55
Adolescence, 53, 148, 179
Adult control, 69
Aggression, 47–48
  counteraggression, 48,
    58, 68
Agnosia, 105
Amphetamines. *See*
    Dextroamphetamine
    sulfate
Anderson, C., 179

Anger, 22, 29–30
Annell, A.L., 155, 179
Anticonvulsant drugs, 89,
    155
Antidepressant drugs,
    150–151
Antihistamines, 154
  diphenhydramine
    hydrochloride, 154
  hydroxyzine
    hydrochloride, 154
  promethazine
    hydrochloride, 154
Anxiety, 22, 30, 31, 35, 37,
    39, 63
  normal, 63

189

Index

Approval, 48
Arnold, L., 148
Attention, 18, 22, 48, 50, 82
   negative, 22, 48
Attention span, 82
Auditory learning, 84, 108

Barbiturates, 92, 151
Bedwetting, 151
Behavior disorders, 79
Behavior modification, 54, 69
Benadryl. *See*
   Diphenhydramine
   Hydrochloride
Bender, L., 152
Benzedrine, 148
Biochemical basis, 101
Bizarre behavior, 40, 86
Blame, 66, 124
Blan, A., 98, 179
Boisterousness, 46
Bond, E.D., 89
Bowlby, J., 36
Bradley, C., 89, 148, 166
Brain damage. *See* Minimal
   brain damage
Brain dysfunction. *See*

Minimal brain
   dysfunction
Brainstem, 101
Brainwashing, 59
Broderick, C.B., 19
Buckley, R.E., 144
Burks, H.F., 148, 180
Bus drivers, 125

Caffeine, 149
Candate nucleus, 100, 144
Cantwell, D.P., 114, 180
Case study, 139
Catecholamines, 101, 102, 150
Chemotherapy. *See*
   Medication
Chess, S., 15
Childhood, 13
Children's games, 2
Chlordiazapoxide, 155
Chlorpromazine, 152
Clements, S.D., 96, 180
Clinging, 23, 38
Clinical management, 37
Coalition, 30, 33
Coffee. *See* Caffeine
Cognition, 114
Collaborate, 12

Companionship, 20
Concentration, 82, 101
Conditioning, 54
Conflict, 22, 31, 38, 48
Conners, C.K., 96, 181
Consequences, 64–67
    natural, 64
Consistency, 65
Controls, 16, 37, 63, 68
    external, 47, 68, 69, 71
    internal, 71, 73
Coordination, 114, 166
Coping, 45, 53, 69, 113
Curiosity, 21
Cytryn, L., 147, 181

David, O., 89, 180
Deafness, 113
    pseudodeafness, 113
Defences, 70
Delinquency, 53
Denhoff, E., 78, 166
Depression, 35, 36
Deprivation, 67
Determinism, 59
Developmental statistics,
    15
Dexedrine. *See*
    Dextroamphetamine

sulphate
Dextroamphetamine
    sulphate, 81, 101, 102,
    143–145, 148
Differential diagnosis, 86
Dilantin, 155
Diphenylhydramine
    hydrochloride, 154
Diphenylhydantoin, 155
Discipline, 48, 57, 71
    negative, 60
    positive, 60
Disruptive behavior, 24, 48,
    68, 69
Distractability, 10, 14
Distraction, 12, 18, 25, 62,
    125
Divorce, 49, 50
Dopamine, 144
Drives, 61, 63
Drug abuse, 134–135
Drugs. *See* Medication
Drug studies, 137
Dyscalculia, 84

Education 2, 14
EEG. *See*
    Electroencephalogram

Index

Eisenberg, L., 146–152, 181
Electroencephlogram, 62, 106
Emotionally disturbed child, 32
Emotions, 68, 113
Encephalitic organic brain syndrome, 88
Endocrine system, 100
Epidemiology, 95–96
Epstein, L.C., 147, 182
Equilibrium, 68
Experience, 49
Exploration, 20
Explosive behavior, 48, 50, 125
Extinction, 54, 63

Fairytales, 77
Family therapy, 42, 53, 115–117
Fantasy, 50, 51, 115
Father, 115, 116
Fire-setting, 164
Flight-fight, 53
Follow-up studies, 167
Food-refusal, 26
Foster home, 117
Franklin, B., 43
Freedom, 59
Freud, S., 1, 58

Friends, 18
Frustration, 20
Fundamentalist, 58

Gibran, K., 109
Growth milestones, 15, 17, 45, 62
Guilt, 31
Habit-patterns, 47
Hammar, S.L., 168
HK. See Hyperkinetic reaction
Hohman, L.B., 88
"Hold-technique," 70
Howlitt, W., 75
Huessy, H.R., 150
Human development, 61
Hydroxyzine hydrochloride, 154
Hyperactive child, 9, 14, 82
Hyperaggressive child, 45, 48, 50
Hyperanxious child, 29–42
Hyperkinetic child, ix, 3–5, 13, 14, 23, 37, 77
Hyperkinetic reaction
    biochemical basis, 101
    definition, 79
    diagnostic work-up, 102
    differential diagnosis, 86, 170

192

epidemics, 97
etiological factors,
    97–102
family, 114
family helps, 118–121
follow-up studies, 167
genetics, 97
medication, 133–157
medication dosages, 147
paradoxical response, 101
physical exam, 104
play therapy, 139
prevalence, 96
prevention, 161, 170–172
prognosis, 161, 164
school, 121
sleep patterns, 146
sociopathy, 169
suggestions, 126–128
symptoms and signs,
    82–83
synonyms, 78–79
teacher, 121

Inconsistency, 53
Independence, 46, 63, 65,
    112
Individual, 3, 12, 59
Individuation, 63
Indoctrination, 59

Indulgent parent, 47, 64
Insecurity, 53
Irritability, 17, 38
Irritants, 48
Isolation, 67

Janeway, C.A., ix, x
Jesuits, 2

Keats, J., 131
Kipling, R., 7

Language, 10, 21
Laufer, M.W., 78, 166
Leadership, 59, 71
Lead poisoning, 89
Learning, 101
Learning disability, 84
Learning theory, 60
Leisure, 14
Liberation, 59
Librium, 155
Limits, 68
Literacy, 77
Lithium carbonate, 102,
    155
Lonely child, 20
Love, 31

Magical thinking, 35
Magoun, H.W., 145–146,
    183

Index

Make-believe, 11
Manic-depressive illness, 102
Manipulate, 53
Mastery, 64, 166
Masturbation, 20–21
Masturbatory equivalents, 21
MBD. *See* Minimal brain dysfunction
Mealtimes, 23–24
Medial forebrain bundle, 100
Medication, 85, 133–157
 anticonvulsants, 89
 Barbiturates, 92, 151
 diagnostic trial, 85
 for hyperkinetic reaction, 134–157
 prejudice against, 85
 school medication consent, 127
 stimulants, 89, 143–149
Mellaril. *See* Thioridazine
Memory, 31
Menkes, M., 168–183
Mental retardation, 89
Methylphenidate, 143–146
Millichamp, J.G., 152
Minimal brain damage, 80
Minimal brain dysfunction, 4, 80, 97, 99, 168, 171, 196
Mourning, 36

Ndika, L.I., 146, 184
Negative attention, 22, 48, 50
Negativism, 53
Neurological pathway, 62
Neurological signs
 soft, 104–106
Newborn, 33, 61
Night terrors, 22
Non-verbal responses, 66–67
Nor-epinephrine, 101

Obscene words, 21
Olds, J., 100, 184
Old Testament, 58
Organic brain syndrome
 encephalitic, 88
 lead poisoning, 89
 post-traumatic, 88
 toxic, 89
Overanxious child, 38, 86

Pain, 34, 64
Parents, 32, 34, 48, 51, 64, 69, 102
Permissiveness, 72

Phenergan. *See*
   Promethazine
   hydrochloride
Phenothiazines, 152–153
   chlorpromazine, 132
   side-effects, 153
   thioridazine, 152
Physician evaluation,
   103–108
Placebos, 137–138
Placement, 117
Play, 11, 19, 113
Post-traumatic   organic
   brain syndrome, 88
Problem analysis, 69
Promethazine
   hydrochloride, 154
Property rights, 18
Psychological testing, 108,
   123, 124
Psychotic child, 32, 39, 86
Punishment, 62–64, 67, 68,
   71
   physical, 65

Rating scale, 90–91
Reassurance, 37–39
Reinforcement, 47, 54, 62
   negative, 62, 66
   positive, 63
Regression, 10

Rejection, 112
Repression, 59
Resentment, 34, 53
Restraint, 70
Reticular activating
   system, 101, 145–146
Rewards, 71
Ritalin. *See*
   Methylphenidate
Rivalry, 31, 50
Robins, L., 168, 185
Romance, 19

Safer, D.J., 97, 148, 185
Scapegoat, 50, 66, 113
Schnackenberg, R.C., 149,
   185
School, 2, 13
School medication consent,
   127
Scott, W., 27
Security, 20, 22
Sedatives, 151
Seizure variants, 87
Self boundaries, 35, 63
Self-confidence, 46
Self-control, 60, 61, 70
Self-discipline, 63, 73
Self-esteem, 63, 66, 166
Self-mutilation, 152
Self-reliance, 73

Index

Self-satisfaction, 63
Separation, 24, 35, 36, 63, 67
Sex organs, 20
Shame, 66
Shelley, E.M., 169, 185
Shy child, 38
Sleep difficulties, 22, 23, 36, 37
Small, A., 146, 185
Smile, 67
Socialization, 13, 46
    primary, 46, 68
    secondary, 46
Solomons, G., 78
Spanking, 65, 66
Special children, 73
Special education, 122, 155
Speech therapy, 19, 108
Speed, 77
Sports, 83
S-R interaction, 54
Stealing, 52, 165
Stereotype movements, 86
Stevenson, R. L., 159
Stimulants, 89, 143–149
    benzedrine, 148
    dextroamphetamine sul-
        fate, 81, 101, 102,
        143–145, 148

methylphenidate,
    143–146
Stimulus, 84
Stress, 24, 38, 67
Substitute teacher, 38
Sydenham's chorea, 88
Symbiosis, 35
Synonyms, 78

Taboos, 47
Tantrums, 20, 22, 38, 113
Teacher, 20, 38, 48, 50, 69, 103
Teacher-healer, 122
Technology, 15
Temperaments, 16
Therapy, family, 42, 53, 115–117
Thioridazine, 152
Thomas, A., 15
Thorazine. See
    Chlorpromazine
Tofranil. See
    Antidepressants
Toilet-training, 61
Towbin, A., 99, 186
Toxic organic brain syn-
    drome, 89
Toys, 20
Tranquillizers, 152

Trust, 151

Unconscious, 59
Underachiever, 51, 83
Unsocialized–aggressive
    reaction, 87
Ventromedial nucleus, 144
Vicarious expression, 50, 52
Victorian era, 57
Violence, 52, 70, 165
Vistaril. *See* Hydroxyzine
    hydrochloride
Visual-perceptual difficulty,
    84, 108

Vocabulary, 21
Vulnerability, 25

War, 22, 70
Weiss, G., 167, 186
Wender Paul, H., 97, 148,
    150, 186
Western culture, 1, 11
Withdrawal, 20, 38, 51
Whitehead, P.L., 155, 186
Wordsworth, W., xi, 1
Wright, A.L., 150

Zrull, J.P., 155, 187